ADAM OSBORNE SPEAKS OUT ON:

The microchip industry: "It has always been full of eccentric personalities. It seems to attract the misfits."

Product transitions: "Switching to a new source of principal income is like climbing a rock face, throwing away your boots halfway up and counting on a new, improved pair for the rest of the climb."

Accounting procedures: "Reserves . . . are an accounting technique which financial people use to make losses from management sins show up in the same time period that the sins were committed. . . . To an accountant the sum of two numbers is any answer you want it to be."

His CEO, Robert Jaunich: "He told me . . . that a man should be measured by how much money he has amassed. To me, that's one of the most incomprehensibly stupid measures of a man anyone could propose."

The future: "The Japanese will enter the market and dominate it . . . Software will be the focus of attention from 1990 into the 21st century."

HYPERGROWTH

"ABSOLUTELY FASCINATING . . . Osborne's famous vision often shines through, together with his wonderful ability to summarize a complex subject in a way that makes it sound obvious."

MicroScope

"Osborne . . . has managed to turn the story of a bankrupt company into a story of personal triumph."

San Jose Mercury News

HYPER-GROWTH

The Rise and Fall of Osborne Computer Corporation

ADAM OSBORNE
& JOHN DVORAK

AVON
PUBLISHERS OF BARD, CAMELOT, DISCUS AND FLARE BOOKS

AVON BOOKS
A division of
The Hearst Corporation
1790 Broadway
New York, New York 10019

Published by arrangement with Idthekkethan Publishing Company
Library of Congress Catalog Card Number: 84-10805
ISBN: 0-380-69960-5

The Idthekkethan Publishing Company edition contains the following Library of Congress Cataloging in Publication data:

Osborne, Adam. Hypergrowth: the rise and fall of Osborne Computer Corporation.

1. Osborne Computer Corporation. 2. Computer industry
—United States 3. Microcomputers. I. Dvorak, John C.
II. Title.
HD9696.C640836 1984 338.7'6100164 84-10805

First Avon Printing, September 1985

Printed in the U. S. A.

OPB 10 9 8 7 6 5 4 3 2 1

To all employees and owners
of Osborne computers

FOREWORD TO THE PAPERBACK EDITION

The original hardcover version of *Hypergrowth* was written based on research conducted between December 1983 and April 1984. A number of lawsuits were filed following the bankruptcy of Osborne Computer Corporation, and additional information started to emerge when depositions were taken from various people in conjunction with these lawsuits beginning in the summer of 1984. Generally, this new information supports and corroborates everything that appears in this book with two notable exceptions:

1. It is suggested in Chapter 9 that in January 1983 Mr. Robert Jaunich, the newly hired President of Osborne Computer Corporation, could have influenced the underwriters in making their decision that Osborne Computer Corporation's public stock offering, originally scheduled for March 1983, should be postponed. Evidence now suggests that the underwriters had come to this conclusion among themselves before they ever met Mr. Jaunich.

2. Chapters 8 and 9 describe a very positive and reassuring letter appearing over Mr. Jaunich's signature which was mailed to investors less than a month before Mr. Jaunich reported a catastrophic change in Osborne Computer Corporation's financial condition. It has now been revealed in depositions that this letter was written by the underwriters and given to Mr. Jaunich to sign. This letter was not written by Mr. Jaunich, nor was the letter his idea.

In Chapter 9, three possibilities are presented:

(a) Jaunich deliberately attempted to manipulate Osborne Computer Corporation financial conditions for his own personal gain
(b) that he was simply incompetent
(c) that he was the innocent victim of runaway circumstances

I stated that I did not believe Mr. Jaunich was incompetent; many readers concluded that I personally believed that Mr. Jaunich manipulated the company for his personal gain. While a number of curious events remain in need of explanation, based on the two facts described in this foreword I now personally believe that Mr. Jaunich did not in any way attempt to manipulate the company's financial condition for his personal gain. I would suggest that readers decide for themselves whether, based on the evidence, Mr. Jaunich was incompetent, or simply an innocent victim of runaway circumstances.

Adam Osborne
January 29, 1985

ACKNOWLEDGMENTS

Originally, this book was intended to be the definitive "What Happened?" story about a company that went bust in the midst of success. To study the company in terms of management flaws, singular blunders, and personality clashes turned out to be nearly impossible. I began by conducting interviews of key people in the company and quickly learned that the entire scene was one big clash. This is not an unusual scenario in the high-tech industries of Northern California.

At Osborne Computer Corporation one of the keys to success was a certain "Us vs Them" mentality that the company used in its dealings with the outside world. Unfortunately the "Us vs Them" mentality was a projection of a "Me vs You" competitiveness that was rampant throughout the company. Interviewing ex-Osborne employees reminded me of the classic old Nast cartoon depicting the Tammany Hall gang. Everyone was pointing a finger at everyone else until a circle was completed creating an infinite loop of accusation.

So we took one perspective—Adam Osborne's. His perspective was the most interesting, the most entertaining and the most complete. This is his story.

A lot of people were of no help and get no thanks from me. Four insiders refused to let me tape them and did not want me to use anything they said or mention their names. Tom Davidson let me tape him but didn't want me to use any of the quotes if Adam had his name on the book. But his information gave me a perspective I needed, so he gets thanked anyway.

I would also like to thank Lee Felsenstein, Barbara Burdick, Georgette Psaris, Fred Brown, Thom Hogen, Bob Marsh, Rich Frank, David

Carlick, Porter Hurt, Paul Freiberger, and George Morrow, for their information, counsel and advice. I would also like to thank John Brockman and Will Hearst for his literary perspectives.

John C. Dvorak
April 5, 1984
Berkeley, CA

I want to thank Cindy Horn, a graduate student at the Business School of the University of North Florida, for four months spent gathering, analyzing and checking information from within and outside of Osborne Computer Corporation. Ron Brown and Mike Anthofer also deserve thanks for their co-operation allowing Cindy Horn and myself access to records within Osborne Computer Corporation.

I want to thank Les Hogan, Jack Melchor and Seymour Rubinstein for taking the time to read critical chapters of this book where they are quoted and referred to extensively.

We did not approach people closer to Mr. Jaunich for interviews, theorizing that Mr. Jaunich would probably threaten litigation in an effort to suppress this book, should he get word of it. Our suspicions were realized when my attorneys received the letter dated April 10th from Mr. Jaunich's attorneys (see next page). A few days later the publisher of this book, a well-known industry name, decided at the last possible minute not to publish it. While not citing Mr. Jaunich's letter specifically, they gave as their reason not wanting to become involved in litigation of any type. I was therefore faced with the choice of turning to another publisher, one less concerned with litigation, or I could publish the book myself. I chose the latter option since any new publisher would be unable to release the book until some time in 1985.

Data presented in this book is the result of exhaustive research efforts, nevertheless, as a cautionary word the reader should be aware that significant confusion surrounded some of the information researched. Although the authors have not knowingly included any errors of fact, that is not to say that some such errors may not have escaped our attention.

Wherever conversations appear in the text they represent my best recollections of what was said. I have not knowingly misrepresented any conversations but it is possible, even probable that others will remember the conversations differently.

Adam Osborne
April 14, 1984
Berkeley, CA

LAW OFFICES OF

PETTY, ANDREWS, TUFTS & JACKSON

A PARTNERSHIP INCLUDING PROFESSIONAL CORPORATIONS

650 CALIFORNIA STREET
THIRTY-FIRST FLOOR
SAN FRANCISCO, CALIFORNIA 94108
(415) 433-1950
TELEX ▯ 9103 722168
CABLE PATNJSF

OF COUNSEL
D. D. HUGHMANICK

SAN JOSE OFFICE
UNION BANK BUILDING
99 ALMADEN BOULEVARD
SUITE 800
SAN JOSE, CALIFORNIA 95115
(408) 998-1952

PALO ALTO OFFICE
755 PAGE MILL ROAD
PALO ALTO, CALIFORNIA 94304
(415) 494-1950

KEITH PETTY*
GEORGE A. ANDREWS, JR.*
ROBERT R. TUFTS*
BARTLETT A. JACKSON*
GEORGE H. COLE, JR.*
TEMPLETON C. PECK*
J. DAVID BLACK*
CHARLES G. STEPHENSON*
JOHN S. SIAMAS*
DAVID T. ALEXANDER*
AUBAN ANN EISENHARDT*
CARL J. STONEY, JR.*
KENNETH J. PHILPOT*
ALLAN J. THOMPSON
MICHAEL J. BAKER
DAVID AYERS THOMPSON
ELLEN McGINTY KING
PETER S. MUNOZ
THOMAS C. DASHIELL
DENNIS V. SWANSON
DEBRA S. BELAGA
EMIL G. PESIRI
JAMES L. McGINNIS
JANICE W. FOX
TWILA L. FOSTER
STEPHANIE E. SMITH
STEPHEN P. PEZZOLA
REBECCA S. EISENBERG
ALAN K. GOLDSTEIN
RICHARD P. MENDELSON
KEITH A. EHRMAN
DONNA M. MEZIAS
JOHN R. HORN
SYLVIA PARK O'NEILL
LUCIA L. BLAKESLEE
*A PROFESSIONAL CORPORATION

April 10, 1984

Leonard G. Weiss, Esq.
Steefel, Levitt & Weiss
San Francisco, California 94111

Dear Mr. Weiss:

We have been advised that Adam Osborne has written and is planning to publish a book about Osborne Computer Corporation that may include libelous material regarding our client, Robert Jaunich. In order to insure that all statements regarding Mr. Jaunich or his role at Osborne are factually correct, we request that Mr. Jaunich be given an opportunity to review the manuscript prior to publication. We ask that you relay this request to any prospective publisher as well as to Mr. Osborne.

This letter is to notify you that, should publication proceed with the inclusion of any libelous material we will initiate legal action on Mr. Jaunich's behalf, seeking compensatory and punitive damages against all responsible parties.

Very truly yours,

PETTY, ANDREWS, TUFTS & JACKSON

Bartlett A. Jackson

BAT/ra
cc: Robert Jaunich

CONTENTS

HYPER-GROWTH

Part I THE RISE

PREFACE

Osborne Computer Corporation was the fastest growing company Silicon Valley had ever seen. It shipped its first computers in July of 1981. September of 1981 saw its first million-dollar month and less than a year later, in August of 1982, it did ten million dollars worth of business in a single month. In its first full fiscal year ending February of 1983 net revenues reached one hundred million dollars. In fact, February of 1983 was the company's best sales month ever. Six months later, in September of 1983, the company filed for bankruptcy amid a roar of publicity that turned the bankruptcy filing into a newsworthy event of nationwide, even worldwide proportions. It was not just the technical press that reported Osborne Computer Corporation's bankruptcy; almost every newspaper in the country carried the story. Even *People* magazine got into the act.

No one, not the company's worst detractor could have predicted such a phenomenal turn of events. A lot of bewildered people are still asking the question: "What happened?"

Press reports following the bankruptcy were generally inaccurate because a great deal went unreported or was misreported, largely for lack of information. No one within the company was talking.

Robert Jaunich then president and chief executive officer, ostensibly adopted a policy of saying nothing to the press. Jaunich's reason, as he explained it to me, was that in the face of anticipated lawsuits resulting from the bankruptcy the less said by everyone the better.

I was also being counciled in the strongest terms by my attorneys to remain silent. My attorneys were worried by the completely distorted view being presented in the press as to who had been running Osborne Computer Corporation. I had founded the company, yet for many months I had played no active role in the company's management. In truth, when the company filed for bankruptcy, I honestly did not know what had happened. But I was not comfortable in my silent role for two reasons: first, so much of what I was hearing simply made no sense; and second, I was simply not used to being silent.

Then in early October of 1983 I got a very conciliatory telephone call from Jaunich. I was invited to dinner at San Francisco's Stanford Court Hotel. There, in the presence of Tom Unterman, the company's attorney and a man trusted by everyone, Jaunich explained the need for total silence on all subjects surrounding Osborne Computer Corporation's bankruptcy. I personally would likely incur enormous litigation costs, Jaunich explained, should I start talking. And above all, I should not be so stupid as to write a book.

I left that dinner with the impression that Jaunich was threatening me into silence. It was on the way home that I decided to write a book about Osborne Computer Corporation. In the course of doing research for this book I would discover for myself what really had happened.

Chapter One THE GREAT IDEA AND HOW IT GREW

The microcomputer industry has always been full of eccentric personalities. It seems to attract the misfits. Few of its leaders would likely have been voted "most likely to succeed."

For instance, there was Lee Felsenstein, who in 1976 designed Processor Technology's SOL, one of the first very popular microcomputers. He is an unrepentant Berkeley radical who once built an electronic bullhorn that could serve alternately as a club in a riot. Then there was Jim Warren, who started the West Coast Computer Faire and watched it grow to a mammoth convention while covering the floor of San Francisco's Brooks Hall on roller skates; and Bill Godbout, a parts supplier and micro maker, who would depart plush hotels after he and his friends had been refused entry into elegant dining rooms because they were wearing jeans, the only class of clothing Godbout or his friends wore.

Even Steve Jobs, one of the Apple founders, was known for his unusual diets and philosophical beliefs. The name of his company, "Apple Computer Corporation," was selected by Steve because at the time he was on a fruit diet. He had given his colleagues an ultimatum to come up with a name they could all agree upon, or he would choose the name of a fruit from his diet. They never met his ultimatum.

I was no stranger to these eccentricities. A chemical engineer by training, I went to work for Shell Chemical Company, only to discover that Shell did not want me. So I went into business for myself—more out of necessity than desire—and by the mid-seventies I was running a small Berkeley-based publishing company that sold books about microcomputers. I saw the enthusiasm of an emerging industry and wanted a part of the action. Often I would show up at the Berkeley Byte Shop with an idea for a new memory card or a new computer. I gave seminars on assembly language programming and was best known for a consumerist column I wrote for *Interface Age* magazine. Above all, I was flamboyant. John Dvorak recalls that I demanded to be the center of attention—not an easy thing to do in the early days of the microcomputer business.

The microcomputer industry began in Albuquerque, New Mexico, where in 1974 a small company called Micro Instrumentation and Telemetry Systems (MITS for short) designed a computer kit. Hobbyists were supposed to buy this unlikely product for $800 and assemble it at home, as they might a Heathkit television set. It was 1975 before MITS actually sold any of its computer kits. They had hoped to sell 800 kits that year, but they were in for a surprise.

Les Solomon, then editor of *Popular Electronics* magazine, got hold of one of the early prototypes and was so taken with it that he featured the MITS computer kit on the January 1975 front cover of the magazine. An immediate boom began. People could now own a cheap computer.

To this day, no one is sure how many kits MITS sold during 1975, but records indicate that on one Friday afternoon in early February of that year 400 orders were placed over the telephone. By late 1975, MITS was one of the largest customers Intel had for its 8080A microprocessor, the computer component of the MITS kit. Intel invented the microprocessor as a component for smart terminals. Ed Roberts of MITS, among others, noticed that it had all the capabilities of a more elaborate central processing unit of a minicomputer. If Intel wasn't going to use it to make a computer, they would.

One of MITS' first important customers was IMS Associates, a California company that wanted to use MITS kits in a business machine—specifically a small computer system to be used by Chevrolet automobile dealers. MITS could not meet the demand for its computer, so IMS Associates built its own copy of the MITS kit—another first in the computer industry. Previously anyone who built a direct copy of someone else's computer could have counted on a lawsuit, but MITS was too inexperienced and too busy to stop and sue.

Here is where I showed up. In December of 1975, I received a telephone call from Bruce Van Natta, a senior manager at IMS Associates. I had never heard of Van Natta or his company, but high technology wasn't the hot area it is today, and any phone call was welcome. Those were the dark days.

Van Netta wanted to know where we could get hold of a book I had written called *The Value of Power.* The book was written in 1972 under contract to General Automation, a minicomputer manufacturer for whom my first company, Osborne and Associates, had provided technical writing services. General Automation used to give this book out free as a promotion piece until 1974 when they hit the skids.

I had written technical documentation for most of the early microprocessor manufacturers, so by mid-1975 not only did I understand these early products well, but I also realized how bright the future was for these products. I therefore decided that Osborne and Associates should become a consulting firm catering to the needs of individuals or companies starting to use microprocessors for the first time.

But even in those early days I was hardly alone. There were already hundreds of individuals and small companies providing similar consulting services. Therefore, to distinguish myself from this throng, I wrote *An Introduction to Microcomputers,* closely patterning it after *The Value of Power*—which had proved enormously popular, even though it had been written as a marketing tool to promote General Automation products.

I first submitted the manuscript for *An Introduction to Microcomputers* to John Wiley & Sons, who seemed like the logical publisher for such a book. They rejected it. Not having the time to hunt all over the publishing world for someone who would accept the manuscript, I decided to print it myself, even though the cost would consume what few assets I then had. So in mid-December 1975, *An Introduction to Microcomputers* became the first book in the world that described microprocessors or microcomputers.

I told Bruce Van Natta that he couldn't get any more copies of *The Value of Power* since General Automation had stopped printing it, and suggested instead *An Introduction to Microcomputers.*

"Even better," Van Natta replied, "show me a copy. I was really looking for a book about microcomputers anyway." So I hurried over to an address in San Leandro, a meager suburb bordering Oakland (itself the undistinguished and ridiculed step-cousin of San Francisco). San Leandro was an unlikely location for the beginning of a revolution. But before I knew it I had sold IMS Associates 10,000 copies of the book at $4 each.

While happy about the sale, I had to wonder what was going on. Who could possibly want 10,000 copies of a book about microprocessor chips—particularly a company operating out of tiny offices in San Leandro. "Either these guys are raving lunatics," I told my secretary, "or they are on to something big."

They were on to something big.

By March of 1976, I had sold 20,000 copies of my book and was into a second printing. Thirteen universities adopted the new book, sight unseen, as a required text. Meanwhile, I was rewriting and improving the text while becoming well known throughout the microcomputer world, since mine was the only book in town. Publishing clearly was a better business than consulting, so I refocused my attention. By the end of 1976, *An Introduction to Microcomputers* had become *Volumes I & II.* I had also written the first of a new series of books called *Programming for Logic Design.* Still, mine were the only microcomputer books available. Not until 1977 did any competing titles appear.

However, a number of magazines were already catering to the microcomputer hobbyist. *Creative Computing* had started publishing in 1974. *BYTE* magazine began in 1975. Early in 1976 Bob Jones turned the Southern California Computer Club's newsletter into his own magazine entitled *Interface Age.* Jones called me shortly after its publication to ask if I would be interested in becoming the magazine's editor.

With my own company to run, I said I was not interested in a full-time job; however, I did agree to provide a monthly column covering microprocessor and microcomputer happenings in the Northwest. Since this geographic territory included Silicon Valley, Jones and I agreed that the column would be called "From the Fountainhead." After all, we rationalized, Silicon Valley was the fountainhead of the microcomputer industry.

To this day, innumerable journalists feel that this title was my first piece of brazen self-aggrandisement.

Originally I had intended to fill my column with descriptions of new microprocessor and microcomputer products; however, before long the entire focus of the column shifted. In those early days the microcomputer industry was filled with amateurs operating companies on a shoestring, since no bank took them seriously. Some of their business practices showed ingenuity, but were nonetheless dubious.

In the absence of venture capital or bank loans, these early entrepreneurs took to funding themselves by advertising products that were still in early stages of design. Customers were required to order by mail with a prepayment. Entrepreneurs used the prepayment to finish designing the product and hopefully could ship it before they got sued. It was not uncommon for companies to have accounts receivable equal to five percent of their accounts payable. It was also not uncommon for people to finally receive shipment of ordered products nine months to a year after their checks had been cashed. If they were very lucky, the product they received worked. At the time, the microcomputer industry was a network of good buddies who, even when they were cashing checks for products that didn't exist, did so out of good-natured necessity. I drew attention to this dubious practice and euphemistically referred to it as "forward financing."

As the microcomputer industry began to mature in 1978, I began to think about ventures other than book publishing.

Most of us understood by then that ours was a growing business. Apple Computer Corporation was already becoming a significant participant, as were Commodore and Radio Shack. McGraw-Hill had approached me to inquire if I was interested in selling my publishing business to them. I was. Even though the company was moderately profitable, the long-range economics were unsound. I was doing close to half-a-million dollars worth of business per month with a total equity base of $3,000 in the company. Furthermore, I knew that sooner or later the large publishers would all start spitting out microcomputer titles, at which time small independent companies with insufficient capital to compete would simply be overwhelmed.

So I agreed to sell my publishing business to McGraw-Hill. The deal was consummated in May of 1979 with a three-year contract to manage and nurture the business until May of 1982. Osborne and Associates was then the dominant publisher of microcomputer books with approximately twenty-five titles.

Slowly McGraw-Hill established its corporate policies within the new subsidiary, which prospered and remains today one of the most profitable divisions of that giant book company.

I personally learned a great deal during those years. Never having had any financial training, I absorbed all I could about the McGraw-Hill systems and procedures.

Meanwhile, the harbinger of Osborne's success, IMS Associates, changed its name to IMSAI and its product—the IMSAI 8080—opened the floodgates. Innumerable little companies sprang up to produce add-on parts for the MITS/IMSAI computer. A small software firm named Digital Research soon designed an operating system named CP/M (Control Program for Microprocessors), which integrated these computers with peripheral mass-storage devices called "floppy disks." Suddenly a standard evolved, but as a standard it would remain in the ranks of the advanced hobbyists. By the time I sold my publishing business, the

CP/M standard was being overtaken by big-time marketeers and the well-organized Apple Computer Corporation.

By 1979 none of the three leading hardware manufacturers—Apple, Commodore, or Radio Shack—subscribed to the microcomputer industry's hobbyist standard. The theme "I do it my way" became more and more prevalent, with the result that software development was retarded. ("Software" represents the instructions used by the computer to do anything at all.) Each machine needed its own unique software. Because there were three leading machines, each program had to be written three times, and a fourth time if a hobbyist standard version was to be available.

Apple and Commodore could not have supported the CP/M standard, since their two products used the 6502 microprocessor, while the hobbyist standard was first based on the 8080A and subsequently on the Z80 microprocessor. Radio Shack could have supported the standard, since their TRS-80 microcomputers were all built around the Z80 microprocessor. However, Radio Shack chose to go its own way with an operating system that differed very slightly from the hobbyist standard, but was proprietary nonetheless.

And yet the CP/M standard did not die. The combined impact of surviving companies—such as North Star, Cromemco, Vector Graphic, and Morrow Designs—was sufficient to keep CP/M alive. This fact did not escape my attention.

By mid-1980, halfway through my management contract period with McGraw-Hill, I realized that I wasn't really interested in staying on as a regular employee. The opportunities working for a large company as a division manager were simply less attractive than the vast potential of the exploding microcomputer industry.

With assets from the successful sale of Osborne and Associates, I looked around for other opportunities. I had the itch to do something new. At first I wanted to build a very inexpensive product that would have been the predecessor of today's home computers, but Clive Sinclair introduced his ZX-80 in Great Britain and I was preempted. I had to build something different.

By this time the microcomputer industry had slowed down. It had entered the temporary period of tranquility that began in 1979 and lasted until late 1980 when the Osborne I and shortly thereafter the IBM PC (personal computer) were introduced. In this intervening period, the industry was dominated by just three manufacturers: Apple, with its Apple

II; Commodore, which had moved forward from the PET to the CBM series of computers; and Radio Shack, with its TRS-80 machines.

I was a student of the microcomputer scene. It dawned on me that price was the real reason for the boom that began with the MITS Altair model. Finally computers were cheap. Also it seemed that people chose microcomputers the way they chose lovers—without logic. This revolution had overtones of an earlier one: the automobile industry. Microcomputers were clearly the American public's next great love affair. But what could I do to compete with Radio Shack and Apple?

The idea was simple: no-frills computing.

This concept can best be summarized with one of my favorite sayings: "Adequacy is sufficient; everything else is irrelevant."

My no-frills concept hypothesized that most microcomputer owners do not begin to use the full capabilities of their computers and are therefore less impressed than they might be with new products that advertise "more power" or "more capabilities." They tend to be far more impressed with lower prices and are amazingly accommodating to the inconveniences that can accompany low cost. Just look at what the early users had to do just to get a system to run: burn their fingers soldering components in place, and then with their burned fingers key programs into the computer using switches.

Another of my tenets was that as IBM has shown time and time again, "To be number one, you don't have to be the best, you don't even have to be good. All that is necessary is that your product be adequate, properly supported, and readily available." IBM proved this point yet again when they introduced their personal computer, a somewhat overpriced and underperforming piece of hardware with little technology to recommend it. Even the much vaunted "16-bit" capability of the IBM PC, based on the 8088 microprocessor, was in reality just marketing hype. The 8088 is about as powerful as the advanced 8-bit Z80 microprocessors in use at that time, and it is still widely used today.

Apple Computer Corporation is another example. Their success has not been based on the technological superiority of their product. On the contrary, the Apple II and IIe have always been somewhat deficient technically. Improbable as it may sound, the Apple II was sold as a business machine when it only displayed forty characters per line on a screen (upper-case letters only), half of the common eighty-character displays offered by similarly priced, competing microcomputers. Yet people bought the technically inferior Apple II, because they were not inconvenienced by its limitations. Technology had nothing to do with Apple

Computer Corporation's success; nor was the company an aggressive price leader. Rather, this company was the first to offer real customer support and to behave like a genuine business back in 1976 when other manufacturers were amateur shoe-string operations.

With these lessons in mind, I designed my computer to include everything that was necessary for low-cost computing and excluded all extras. The philosophy was that if 90 percent of users' needs were adequately covered, the remaining 10 percent of the market could be sacrificed.

In 1980 microcomputers were generally configured like the Apple II: innumerable boxes that had to be plugged together in a maze of wiring and cables. If the market was to grow, it would have to rely on customers who would plug a computer into the wall, as they might a toaster. The wires and cables had to go so the new computer could come integrated into a single package.

I decided to build the smallest possible package, given the components then available; thus was born the idea of the "portable computer." And if the product was going to be carried from table to table or from office to office, why not let people travel with it? I researched the maximum dimensions most airlines allowed for carry-on baggage so the package would fit under an airline seat.

The Osborne I was thus created. It included the following features:

1. The central processing unit chosen for the Osborne I was the Z80, the most popular and inexpensive at that time.
2. CP/M was the operating system.
3. 64K bytes of memory (1K equals 1,024) were provided, the maximum usable by the Z80 short of playing tricks in hardware design. One byte is roughly equivalent to one letter of the alphabet or to one numeric digit.
4. The Osborne I had to have two disk drives. It is very difficult with just one to copy programs or data from one disk to another. The simplest single-density, single-sided disk drives were selected, since there were innumerable unknown questions associated with disk-drive reliability in a portable environment. Unfortunately, a single-density, single-sided disk drive has a maximum storage capacity of approximately 100,000 characters of information, which for most applications is a bare minimum bordering on being inadequate. This decision would come back to haunt me in the months to come.
5. A standard typewriter keyboard was included. Other manufactur-

ers had attempted to cut cost by using glorified calculator keyboards, but these had invariably met with strong customer resistance.

6. Two standard connectors (known to the technical world as "parallel and serial interfaces") were provided for printers and other external accessories.

7. For convenience, pockets were included below the disk drives so users could store diskettes in them and avoid having to carry around an extra box or suitcase.

8. A five-inch screen was built into the Osborne I. I selected this small screen because I wanted to make the entire unit as small as possible. In the event that the screen proved too small, a connector was included so that a larger external screen could be attached. Unfortunately, the small screen could not display eighty readable characters on one line. Fifty-two characters were displayed (twelve more than the Apple II), but the line could be longer, with the fifty-two characters acting as a window on the longer line. This is another decision that would have repercussions in the next few months.

My greatest coup was the software bundled with the Osborne I. While today the feat might appear to be an awesome piece of business acumen, at the time it was both obvious and easy to negotiate because the CP/M market was struggling.

A number of software companies that had developed CP/M-based products suddenly found themselves selling into a shrinking segment of the market, since their software would not run on microcomputers built by the three emerging industry leaders. Therefore, they were frantic to breathe new life into the CP/M market, and they were very ready to deal.

The choice of what software to include was also straightforward. Industry surveys had shown that more than eighty percent of the market at that time used their microcomputers for word processing and/or for spreadsheet applications—an explosive market that Bob Frankston and Dan Bricklyn had opened up with their revolutionary software package, VisiCalc. And since a lot of people still programmed their own microcomputers, I chose the two most popular programming languages: MBASIC from Microsoft, and CBASIC, the brain child of Gordon Eubanks.

There was only one word processor to consider: WordStar. It was without a doubt the industry leader among CP/M-based word processing systems. The electronic spreadsheet was harder to come by, since there were no VisiCalc equivalent programs running on CP/M-based machines—and Visi-Corp was reluctant to deal with me. I subsequently discovered why: they had charged large fees to Radio Shack and Hewlett Packard (reputedly $1 million each) to generate CP/M equivalents of VisiCalc for these manufacturers' machines. I certainly could not match these figures. I therefore went to Richard Frank, president of Sorcim and asked if he would write a CPM-based Visi-Calc-type program for me. He agreed. I gave Frank the specifications I was looking for, which were basically VisiCalc with a few added capabilities, and thus SuperCalc came into existence.

With the concept clear in my mind, I set out to put the pieces together. Here is a summary of the deals I negotiated:

1. I bought an unlimited CP/M license for $55,000, the going rate at that time. It was no special deal, but I was one of the last to get this rate before Digital Research changed its policies and discontinued selling unlimited licenses.
2. I traded unlimited licenses to bundle CBASIC and MBASIC with Osborne computers. Each traded for 2,875 shares of OCC stock, which at the time represented approximately 2.5 percent of the company's outstanding shares. I made my deal with Gordon Eubanks for CBASIC and with Microsoft for MBASIC.
3. WordStar was a little more complicated, and the terms of the deal were never to be disclosed.
4. For SuperCalc I paid the development costs, which came to approximately $20,000—a far cry from the million dollars approximately that VisiCorp would have charged. I got unlimited rights to distribute SuperCalc with my computer; however, Sorcim retained rights to sell the program anywhere else, under the condition that he was to repay the $20,000 development costs out of future revenues. Sorcim also got 4,000 shares of stock for additional software help.

Thus, the total expense to Osborne Computer Corporation for its bundled software included the fixed payments to Digital Research and Sorcim, MicroPro's fees, plus the manufacturing cost of diskettes and documentation—less than $10 per computer.

Although these software agreements were not concluded until early 1981, negotiations began along with all other plans for the Osborne I in the summer of 1980. At that time I was still working for McGraw-Hill, who knew of my extracurricular activities and of my intention to leave once my contract period ended in May of 1982.

Osborne Computer Corporation came into being early in 1980 as a Subchapter S California Corporation with the name "Brandywine Holdings." But by mid-1980 the company still had no employees—just me working evenings, and Lee Felsenstein, the old Berkeley radical who started work in July of 1980 as a consultant designing hardware. I had known Lee since 1976, when he had done some technical consulting for Osborne/McGraw-Hill. Since Lee worked a few blocks away from Osborne/McGraw-Hill's offices, and since he was well qualified, he seemed the ideal candidate to design the electronics for my new computer. I agreed to pay Lee subsistence wages together with 25 percent of the new company's stock.

It was also in the summer of 1980 that I went to Jack Melchor and told him about the new project. I had met Melchor through Les Hogan, one of Silicon Valley's founding fathers. While chairman of Fairchild Semiconductor, Hogan had read my first book, *An Introduction to Microcomputers*. Impressed with this book, he had summoned me to his audience. I was in awe of this great man when I approached this first meeting in early 1976. Subsequently we became good friends and remain so today. Hogan belonged to various investment groups headed by Melchor. I advised Melchor on possible microcomputer investments, and we also became good friends.

I think that Hogan and Melchor represent the finest elements of the Silicon Valley entrepreneurial culture. Both are shrewd businessmen, but they are also two of the finest human beings I have ever met. They are warm, honest, and forthright. They assume they are dealing with honest people and their integrity is virtually transparent. This was consistent with the environment I had encountered everywhere else in Silicon Valley.

During the summer of 1980, Melchor offered me advice and counsel on product design, pricing, and staffing. At the end of 1980 he also invested $40,000 of seed money out of a fund under his control. By then I had spent approximately $100,000 for my new venture. Up to the end of 1980, $140,000 invested had created a working prototype microcomputer capable of running some software. It was time to incorporate. Melchor insisted that the company's name be changed to Osborne Computer Corporation to capitalize on name recognition. Under this name the company was incorporated in the first days of 1981.

Thus Osborne Computer Corporation was born.

Chapter Two THE CORPORATE LAUNCH

A burgeoning "high-tech" hardware company must take these four steps: First, a prototype product must be designed and built. Second, venture capital must be raised. Third, personnel must be hired. Fourth, visibility must be acquired for the company and a consumer base must be developed.

A well-known entrepreneur with a successful track record can often get so-called "seed venture capital" to back an idea, but for the rest of us just a gleam in the eye is not good enough. Venture capitalists like to see, touch, and feel before they invest. They may even react positively to the smell of poverty. It means you thought enough of your idea to back it with your own meager resources.

In 1980 I was best known for my "From the Fountainhead" column, which did not constitute a successful track record. Nor did it qualify me as a well-known entrepreneur, which is why I had to pay for the design and construction of the Osborne I prototype myself, with a little help from Jack Melchor.

My original business plan anticipated the unit shipments shown in Table 1. I used VisiCalc to prepare my original business plan; hence the precise-looking numbers beyond September. It is easy to spot tables that have been prepared using a spreadsheet program; they're the ones with numbers increasing monthly by some fixed-growth factor. Growth factors are easy to use when working with spreadsheets, and they create impressive tables. Too many zeros scream out that the table is contrived.

To fund this growth I managed to raise $900,000 in February and March of 1981. Of this just $340,000 came from venture capital sources, all with Melchor's help. The rest of the money came from my friends and me, and even raising this paltry sum was no picnic. Those were the first days of working with an empty pain in the pit of my stomach as I added up $10,000 here and $20,000 there to see if VisiCalc felt I finally had enough to meet my cash-flow projections.

Table I **Initial plan for Osborne I unit shipments, January 1981.**

1981 Computer Unit Sales		*1982 Computer Unit Sales*	
June	200	January	2687
July	400	February	2902
August	1200	March	3135
September	1440	April	3385
October	1728	May	3656
November	2074	June	3949
December	2488	July	4265

In retrospect, $900,000 was a pitiable sum—woefully insufficient to launch a project of Osborne Computer Corporation's magnitude. When I invited Jerry Anderson of Two Pi Corporation to my new bachelor condo-warming party, he commented, encouragingly:

''To pull this one off, you'll have to be a magician.''

But $900,000 was all the money I could raise at the time. I knew I would have to run the company on it until August or September.

The initial Board of Directors included myself, Jack Melchor, Seymour Rubenstein (founder of MicroPro), Les Hogan, Richard Frank (of Sorcim), Robert Bily, and Tony Bergis.

Bergis was a manufacturer's representative who came to sell and stayed to invest. Robert Bily represented his own investment and that of his brother-in-law.

Gordon Eubanks (of CBASIC fame) and Bill Gates of Microsoft were both offered seats on the Board, but declined, citing potential conflicts of interest. Richard Frank soon resigned from the Board for the same reason, and perhaps because he found himself in frequent conflict with Lee Felsenstein. Frank was replaced in September of 1981 by Ken Oshman, president of Rolm Corporation.

I began looking for personnel in December of 1980, while Osborne Computer Corporation was still ''Brandywine Holdings'' and the Osborne I computer was a jumble of printed circuit boards and wires spread across bench space in inelegant accommodations. The space used to create the new computer was shared with Berkeley's electronic anarchist underground, members of the "Community Memory Project" whose avowed goal was to bring computing to the people by placing a network of computer terminals in every imaginable public location.

I was still working long hours at Osborne/McGraw-Hill, then at the low point of its fortunes following the McGraw-Hill acquisition; Osborne/McGraw-Hill had been losing money since May of 1979. (A turnaround to profitability did not occur until early 1981.) In late 1980 the parent company's management reacted to this division's unprofitability by making indecisive noises about reorganization, a sell-off of the division or an early termination of the earn-out period. As a consequence, a number of key Osborne/McGraw-Hill employees resigned, compounding my day-to-day problems.

Given these time-consuming difficulties at Osborne/McGraw-Hill, it was imperative that I find a good general manager for the new computer company. Someone with a manufacturing background had to be hired right away. Not only did I lack manufacturing experience, but I also knew I could count on exciting times during the balance of my contract with McGraw-Hill through May 1982. For more than a year after the new computer company's formation, the general manager would have to run day-to-day operations.

The hiring of this individual was the first major obstacle I encountered. Initially I went to a number of personal acquaintances who had the credentials, but they all turned me down flat. They, like Jerry Anderson, were unanimously skeptical of the basic concept and of my ability, as an ex-journalist, to get the project off the ground.

I eventually had to run a blind advertisement in the *Wall Street Journal.* Since the ad was to appear only in California, the folks at the *Wall Street Journal* reran it in their *National Business Employment Weekly,* as is their wont. An enormous pile of dismal resumes soon started to arrive, interspersed with the occasional gem. I soon learned to save time by throwing away, unread, all responses that cited the *National Business Employment Weekly,* a periodical that surely must be the scourge of all personnel managers. The few well-qualified respondents declined to participate, again citing their lack of confidence in the very idea of a portable microcomputer.

But a candidate was eventually found via the *Wall Street Journal* ad. His name was Tom Davidson. On December 15, 1980, Tom started work as the new company's vice president and general manager; he was also the company's first full-time employee, since Lee Felsenstein was still acting as a consultant. Felsenstein remembers best the appearance of Davidson's resume; it appeared to have been typed using an old manual typewriter.

Tom Davidson grew up in Brooklyn, New York. And this famous borough has never exported a more obvious product of its unique environment. Physically, Davidson looked as though he was well equipped to survive a Brooklyn upbringing. He looked and sounded tough. Davidson was a man blessed with immense "street smarts" and boundless energy. Mostly self-educated, Davidson had a depth of native cunning that gave him a gut understanding of issues. He had run a New York taxicab company at one time, a job for which he must have been well suited. His most recent job, however, had been with the West Coast branch of an East Coast company whose management spoke in glowing terms of his ability to run a manufacturing operation.

Georgette Psaris, then only 25, was the next key manager to join Osborne Computer Corporation. She had worked at Osborne and Associates as a sales representative prior to the McGraw-Hill acquisition. She quickly rose to become director of sales and marketing, a post she held until early 1981, when she quit during the period of unrest. After interviewing with a number of companies (including McGraw-Hill in New York), Psaris accepted the position of vice president of sales and marketing at Osborne Computer Corporation. She reported directly to me. The rest of the company reported to Davidson.

Most of my successes have really been successes of an Osborne-Psaris team. I have always known what needed to be done; Psaris knew how to turn vision into reality. I challenged and inspired people; Psaris blended them into a working team, in the absence of which no amount of excitement will produce results. These skills she learned at Osborne/McGraw-Hill, and exercised at Osborne Computer Corporation. From a standing start, in one year she built a sales and marketing organization that propelled the company to its magnificent heights.

Psaris also was the perfect match for Davidson. It would be the beginning of a long battle. He considered her to be an amateur, but Psaris above all people could stand toe-to-toe with Davidson in a confrontation.

Lynn Hagen was another early member of the founding team. To me he epitomized the "golden boy." He was young (at the time just 24), handsome and blond. Lynn somehow surrounded himself with a feeling of vitality. Reporting to Psaris, he was assigned the task of preparing the "ideal" dealer program. Based on this, Osborne Computer Corporation would roll out its new product and grab shelf space among America's best computer stores. Working as a consultant, Hagen had previously established a very successful telemarketing operation for Osborne/McGraw-Hill. Hagen was a major early investor in Osborne Computer Corporation, along with his brother-in-law Robert Bily, who represented both of their investments on the company's Board.

I had met Barbara Burdick almost a year earlier, in March of 1980, at the West Coast Computer Faire. She then worked for TNW Corporation, a small company making communications equipment for Commodore microcomputers. Although Barbara lived in San Diego, we became very good friends.

By late 1980 Barbara had decided to move on from her position at TNW. Since most of the high-tech job opportunities were in the San Francisco Bay Area, she decided to relocate north in January of 1981. Barbara Burdick is a charmer. Where Psaris confronted Davidson head-on, Barbara somehow always brought him around to her way of thinking without a fight. With these admirable qualifications, Barbara agreed to act as a public relations consultant to Osborne Computer Corporation for three months while looking for a full-time job elsewhere. She received a number of interesting offers, but when her consulting contract ended in April, she accepted the Osborne Computer Corporation offer.

Annette Truesdell responded to a newspaper ad. In March she was hired to handle customer and dealer relations, two areas where the new company grew to be particularly strong. Annette had worked for many high-tech companies at a variety of jobs with increasing marketing and customer service responsibility.

Together with Lee Felsenstein, Curt Ingraham and Pat McGuire constituted the infant company's engineering department. Curt was manager of the technical staff at Osborne/McGraw-Hill, and Pat was a member of Curt's technical staff. Both left at about the same time as Psaris, during the turmoil of late 1980 and early 1981.

Knowing the importance of technical documentation, we hired Mike Iannamico in February 1981 to start writing the Osborne I user manual, many months before the product's introduction. Iannamico and I were supposed to write the documentation together; unfortunately, when it came to the amount of work I could undertake, my ambitions frequently exceeded reality, and Iannamico finished writing most of the documentation himself.

Marlene Tanner joined Osborne Computer Corporation in January of

1981 as my administrative assistant. She was perfect for me—kind of a Radar O'Reilly of the TV show *MASH.* She had the telepathy and precognition that a good administrative assistant needs to know what she is *not* being told and to foretell the critical events that her boss only thought he remembered telling her.

The new company's offices into which Davidson moved in December 1980 consisted of one room on loan from Sorcim—then a very small software company. This was where Richard Frank and his cohorts created SuperCalc, the spreadsheet program that I would bundle with the new computer. One room would not last long, and Davidson's first priority was to find more permanent work space for the company.

Felsenstein, Psaris, and I lived in Berkeley, and Davidson lived near San Jose; we agreed to look for space midway between these two locations, in the general vicinity of Hayward or San Leandro. Davidson ultimately found a building in the Eden Landing Industrial Complex in Hayward. The building was just a shell, but the owners agreed to let the new company's few employees move in while the inside was being completed around them. The city of Hayward was proud of their new high-technology firm. I never was able to persuade Hayward's city fathers that only a map and a piece of string led us to choose their city as the site for Osborne Computer Corporation's headquarters.

In the middle of January 1981, the first few Osborne Computer Corporation employees settled into the empty shell of a building that became the company's first headquarters. (Davidson used to park his car on the spot that eventually became my office.) Everyone attempted to make telephone calls around the schedule of construction workers driving rivets into concrete walls. On cold days most people's fingers were numb by late afternoon when I finally showed up, having completed my day at Osborne/McGraw-Hill. Of course, we all look back on those early days in a half-finished building as the company's finest hours.

In these quarters we prepared for the West Coast Computer Faire, where at the end of March Osborne Computer Corporation would announce its product. Psaris was putting together her team. Burdick cultivated the press, telling them under nondisclosure what we were doing and when they could write about it. The engineering crew worked night and day trying to build a few working prototype computers. By mid-March the job was completed—just days before the Faire opened. Four trade magazines illustrated our product on their front covers. It would have been unspeakable if, after preparing so much publicity, we had had nothing to show.

The price finally agreed upon was "$1795." It was at the high end of price ranges that had been contemplated and had an awkwardness to it that people would remember. At that price we would make a lot of money, providing Davidson could batter vendors into submission and buy parts for the aggressively low prices I had specified.

For Osborne Computer Corporation, the show was an astounding success and an enormous morale booster. The industry was still in transition, and many exhibitors were small-time operators working out of curtain-draped booths with inelegant, show-provided cardboard pinned to the rear curtain to tell the world who they were. But not Osborne. Spending a little of my $900,000, we built a plexiglass booth that towered toward the ceiling, projecting the new company's "flying O" logo as a beacon and landmark across the show floor.

More than a dozen stories about the introduction appeared in the West Coast Computer Faire issue of various trade periodicals. For a company with neither a history nor a product, this was a remarkable achievement. A large number of people stopped me at that show to ask who was handling my public relations. The truth was Burdick and I—we were handling the job ourselves.

The prototype Osborne I, as introduced at the West Coast Computer Faire, was an ugly machine inside a heavy aluminum case. The metal case was used because no one thought a switching power supply (the kind that generates very little heat) would be available within the targeted price range, and any other power supply generated more heat than any plastic case could dissipate. However, a vendor approached Davidson at the West Coast Computer Faire and offered him a low-cost switching power supply. In spite of the cost being more than I had budgeted for power supplies, it was reasonable nevertheless.

The metal prototype Osborne I also had a display that swayed. A gentle ripple moving through text on the screen was euphemistically called the "Hawaiian effect" by employees manning the West Coast Computer Faire booth.

Ugly and hot or not, the computers worked. Our booth drew huge crowds, largely because of the announced retail price: $1795 was roughly half of what any other microcomputer cost, including the same software. An equivalent Apple II with the same amount of software cost over $3000.

At $1795, some Computer Faire attendees still scoffed at the small screen and sewing machine case, but they knew it was a steal with all of the software we had thrown in for nothing. Before an audience that overflowed into adjacent halls, I issued my challenge to the industry: "Do as I have done or perish!"

We were on a roll. And we knew it.

It was an unlikely crew issuing such a challenge to the industry, promising machines to be on dealers' shelves by June: a columnist, an ex-taxicab operator, and a collection of hugely enthusiastic ex-juveniles. Small wonder that some who heard and saw us were skeptical. But the Osborne I was the undeniable hit of the show.

A "financial professional" was hired in February of 1981. During the West Coast Computer Faire, this poor fellow, on whom we will bestow the pseudonym "Ben Counter," had his first "high-tech" experience. It would have been enough to unnerve anyone with an accounting mind. Almost every nonclerical Osborne employee was at the Faire when Steve Jobs of Apple Computer Corporation telephoned.

When informed that neither I nor any other Osborne executive was in the office, Steve spoke to Ben Counter. His message to Ben was: "Tell Adam he's an asshole."

After consulting gravely with Marlene Tanner, Ben agreed that she should be the one to pass on this horrifying message.

"There's a funny message for you," Marlene told me that evening. "It's from Steve Jobs of Apple. He says you're an— asshole."

Poor Ben was awestruck when, instead of being annoyed, I collapsed into waves of uncontrollable laughter. But worse, I repeated Steve Jobs' message to more than five hundred people at the Faire the next day. It was, according to me, the company's first official response from the competition.

And then the Faire was over. It was time to deliver on our promises. No one within the company doubted it would be done.

Having found a switching power supply, Davidson went to work acquiring a vacuum-formed plastic case. It was the only type he could obtain for the Osborne I in the short time before product shipments were to begin in June; otherwise the company would be out of money. It is probably fortunate that this change was made. An egg could have been cooked in the disk pocket of an early metal-case prototype Osborne I computer.

Davidson set about negotiating contracts with vendors to provide needed components. He was able to force substantial price concessions, both in consequence of his personality and the prevailing market conditions, which were slack.

"I got my jock strap flyin' in the wind for a million dollars!" he would plead as he beat a few extra pennies per component out of some poor, harried sales representative, while he uttered phrases understood only by those who knew and loved him.

But much to everyone's amazement, Davidson discovered that major manufacturers like Apple Computer Corporation and Radio Shack appeared to be paying more for components than necessary (although definitive proof was never obtained). Normal price erosion being strong anyway, other buyers had not aggressively enough driven prices down further, which is why Davidson was able to buy components for less than our competitors realized.

Some months later at the National Computer Conference in Chicago, Apple Computer Corporation's buyer confronted Davidson at the Osborne booth. He showed Davidson Apple Computer Corporation's assumed bill of materials for the Osborne I. Holding the proffered piece of paper at arm's length, Davidson scanned the numbers, a slow and self-satisfied smile creeping across his face.

"This is what you guys're payin'?" he asked with his distinctive New York accent.

The bill of materials showed just how much Apple was overpaying for a number of components, or presumed Osborne was paying at that time. For example, Davidson was buying disk drives at $80 each—$10 less than Apple assumed.

Davidson was an enormous asset to Osborne Computer Corporation in those early days. Treating vendors, employees, and anyone else who got in his way with gruff abruptness, he ran a tight operation and obtained extraordinary price concessions from vendors. As long as instinct was sufficient, he achieved much and solved problems with remarkable efficiency. He did not like spending money and took personal pride in every dollar he saved—which was just as well, since my $900,000 was shrinking fast.

From January 1981 until the first Osborne I was shipped on June 30 of that year, everything Davidson touched went well. The timely introduction of the Osborne I can be credited largely to his hard work. But its extraordinary acceptance by a dealer network—few of whom had ever seen a production model—was the work of Psaris and Hagen.

Before the West Coast Computer Faire was over, Osborne Computer Corporation had already gone a long way toward completing step four of their start-up plan: the company had certainly acquired visibility and was also well on its way toward establishing a customer base.

The first Osborne dealer, the Digital Deli, had had a booth at the Faire directly across from ours. During the show they took ninety orders for July delivery. On June 30, 1981, Osborne Computer Corporation shipped its first computer—to Gerald Wright of the Digital Deli in Mountain View, California. The computer's serial number was 000001. Gerald Wright still has that computer today.

A QUESTION OF MEDIA

When Osborne Computer Corporation announced its new product, it seemed imperative to induce a deluge of media coverage, since there were already innumerable other small companies building microcomputers, mostly selling at low volume. Our new company had to differentiate itself from this throng of little-known, small-time players. We could make it only if consumers perceived our new company as among the industry leaders. With strong press coverage, product demand and sales volumes should prove excellent, in which case dealers would also clamor for our product.

Working with Barbara Burdick, I had no trouble orchestrating the media attention. I have always believed that the best advertising is free advertising, easily generated by turning press releases into human interest stories. Accordingly, all product announcements became industry challenges, laced with a "critic takes on the industry" theme. The press loved it.

The key to working well with the press is understanding that journalists have a product to sell: a story. Help them write a good story—one that is widely read—and they'll love you for it. Journalists are, after all, only human—and good stories advance journalistic careers. Few journalists specifically look for "good" or "bad" stories; they look instead for "interesting" stories. You and the reporter are actually co-workers. Treat the reporter as an enemy, and he or she will fulfill your expectations: after all, faced with a hostile or defensive co-worker, what other choice is there but to become defensive oneself? Thus, I have always given journalists my time, working symbiotically to each do the other some good. Knowing what it is I want printed, I look at the story from the reporter's viewpoint and structure it to sell.

My theory further states that waves of free publicity are best created by generating saturation media coverage for short periods of time. It is far better to have ten stories in one week than one story a week for ten weeks. Each wave of stories attracts the attention of one higher media level; reporters watch, and in the lull following each wave write the "exclusive" stories that invariably appear together and cause the next wave.

My "wave theory" of publicity has another, less obvious advantage. Media stories are initiated by knowledgeable professionals who report events and express useful opinions arising from their base of knowledge, but invariably subsequent press coverage is the work of less-informed journalists who are in mortal terror of penning a harsh statement that they might be called on to defend. So they rehash previous stories, adding little or nothing new. A good first wave of publicity thus gets reported and re-reported, wave after wave, by this legion of writers whose writings attest to their fear that someone might suspect the truth: that they really do not understand what they are writing about. And so they write "safe" stories, simply agreeing with what was previously reported. To the extent that any new information is added in the subsequent waves of press coverage, it tends to be a marginally accurate embellishment designed to bolster the original sentiment.

Unfortunately, a wave of bad publicity gets re-reported in waves much the same way—and bad news out of control can ruin a company.

Apart from a brief mention in *Vantage Research,* an obscure industry newsletter, not one word about Osborne Computer Corporation's new product was printed until Ed Schaeffer, one of the country's best-informed journalists broke the story in the *Wall Street Journal* one week before the 1981 West Coast Computer Faire. One paragraph in the technology column of the second section's front page paralyzed Osborne Computer Corporation's telephone switchboard. It was many days before callers stopped getting a busy signal when they phoned in. During those few days, anyone wanting to call out had to hover over a telephone with the receiver off the cradle and jump on any line that cleared.

This early wave of publicity was followed by the expected lull, which was broken, again as expected, by a simultaneous crop of short, skeptical articles in newspapers and business periodicals. Then came the next lull while the financial community watched. When the company achieved a totally unexpected level of success, longer and more favorable articles appeared in business magazines. As I will describe in a later chapter, careful juggling of interview schedules enabled me to ensure that long, favorable articles would simultaneously appear in *Fortune* and *Business Week* magazines, in February 1982, which in turn attracted the attention of the *60 Minutes* television program managers as well as *Time* and *Newsweek* magazines.

When creative publicity is orchestrated with a creative advertising campaign, the effect is greater than the sum of its parts.

Even by the fall of 1981, it seemed as though nothing could hurt sales. Engineering problems and management disputes that swirled around the Davidson-Psaris camps were buried under an avalanche of orders and a hugely successful advertising campaign—a forte of the company, thanks to Psaris working closely with a then-unknown advertising firm, David Carlick Advertising.

In 1979, while operating virtually on his own, Carlick had done some work for Georgette Psaris at Osborne/McGraw-Hill. After joining Osborne Computer Corporation, she retained him as the new company's full-time advertising agency.

The keys to Carlick's success were, first, his enthusiasm for the product concept and, second, the fact that he was given a lot of creative leeway. His professional structure was loose, and creativity was more important to him than contracts.

Osborne Computer Corporation's first two campaigns are probably among the best remembered in the microcomputer industry. Prior to product shipment the slogan was:

"It was inevitable."

This excellent "preintroduction" slogan said it all. There was nothing particularly revolutionary about the Osborne I: someone inevitably would bundle together the hardware and software most commonly used by microcomputer owners into one "friendly" package. The second slogan, however, is probably the better known:

"The guy on the left doesn't stand a chance."

This slogan appeared below a picture of two people: the one on the left carried a briefcase while the one on the right carried an Osborne I. It appealed directly to the fear of obsolescence so prevalent among professionals at that time. I backed it up on the lecture circuit, where I would finish many public addresses by stating:

"If you work with numbers or words and you are not using a microcomputer, then you are working on borrowed time."

Another frequent comment I made was:

"You may be the first or the last to get a microcomputer, or you can get a real estate license." This second quote sounded good but was inaccurate. Real estate salespeople were also early microcomputer users.

These advertising campaigns were the products of Psaris' bright ideas which, working closely with Carlick, became reality. Coupled with my public lectures, the Psaris-Carlick advertising was an important component in gaining quick brand identification in the public eye. The advertising messages were designed to strike an immediate responsive chord and were backed up by my public statements stressing the underlying human trends that were sustaining the microcomputer industry. But my public statements were always deliberately phrased provocatively enough to attract media attention. Thus *Business Week* wrote about the company's early success under the slogan "From Brags to Riches," while the *New York Times* coined the heading: "Brat Makes Good." It was all superb media coverage. The public loved it, and they remembered our name when they entered the computer store.

A QUESTION OF RETAILING

Following the introduction of the Osborne I at the West Coast Computer Faire, the company had to make its first retailing decision. Should we use distributors or sell directly to dealers?

With no dissension, we resolved not to use distributors, but instead to directly support the domestic dealer network. It is my belief that distributors have a diminishing role to play in the microcomputer industry, where cost is everything. The additional margin inserted by distributors increases retail prices, and nothing they do can compensate for the sales erosion resulting from this price increase.

Consider two of the most common arguments used by distributors to justify their existence in the microcomputer industry: distributors finance dealer inventory, and they allow dealers to offer a wider range of product.

Distributors do in fact finance dealer inventory by offering overnight delivery from stock, so the dealer need only own showroom demonstration units. The problem here is that the distributor has to finance his inventory, just as the dealer would, and this finance charge is passed on to the dealer within the distributor's markup. So why shouldn't the dealer finance his inventory directly? Simply because the dealer is financially too weak to qualify for such financing (in which case he can't last long in the increasingly competitive microcomputer retail marketplace anyway).

Carrying several brands of product, the distributor does allow dealers to offer their customers more choices. But a small dealer can't possibly know too many different microcomputer systems well enough to support them all. (Big dealers can't either.) If the dealer does not offer competent support, then the customer might as well buy from 47th Street Photo in New York, where he'll get a great price with no pretense of after-sales service or support. In 1981 it was surprisingly easy to acquire shelf space in dealer showrooms. It probably still is today.

It is amazing how few manufacturers in the microcomputer industry understand that computer stores, like any other retail business, only stock products for which there is a demonstrable customer demand. There is no truth to the rumor that by gaining computer store shelf space a manufacturer can create sales. Computer dealers never have and probably never will create demand for any of the products they carry. Creating consumer demand has always been and will continue to be the manufacturer's responsibility. Dealers carry products for which someone else has already created consumer demand—with just one proviso: the profit margin must exceed some minimum threshold. Dealers stock these products for only as long as the consumer demand remains.

Dealers have no loyalty independent of consumer demand; nor can they afford the altruism of any such loyalty. Therefore, manufacturers must base their advertising and public relations campaigns on creating consumer awareness and demand for product. Dealers only run "me too" advertising, the theme of which is: "Hey! I have the hot product, buy it from me, because . . ." and then the dealer's own message begins.

Stores' shelves are particularly volatile; it is as important for the dealer to carry the "hot" product as it is for the manufacturer to see his product carried. Thus, manufacturers are either turning dealers away or courting them with little success. There is almost no middle ground, and in a matter of weeks a manufacturer can swing from one position to the other.

Gaining dealer shelf space in 1981 was made even easier because Apple Computer Corporation's dominant market position had caused it to take a very cavalier attitude toward dealers, many of whom were carrying Apple products for the single reason that they had nothing else to sell. Radio Shack sold strictly through their own outlets. And Commodore's dealer relations since they first started building microcomputers in 1976 have been atrocious enough to make anyone, even Apple, appear saints by comparison. Commodore's lack of support and capricious policy changes meted out to their dealers leads one to the conclusion that Apple could not have done a better job of designing a policy to sabotage their rival's dealer network. Eventually Commodore turned to mass-market channels for the bulk of its sales.

Nevertheless, dealer-product dynamics allowed both Apple Computer Corporation and Commodore to be successful despite their antagonism toward virtually any dealer who ever carried their product. Dealers will curse a manufacturer and still order his product if customer demand remains. Dealers will also drop a product with equal speed when customer demand disappears, irrespective of whether or not the manufacturer treated them well.

Today I believe that manufacturers should be totally self-serving in their dealer relations, giving the dealer the bare minimum acceptable deal. Anything more is ill-spent money that will never generate higher sales.

But this was not my thinking when Georgette Psaris and Lynn Hagen worked at putting together the "ideal" dealer program. Generous profit margins were offered, ranging between 35 to 42 percent of the listed retail price. Dealers had thirty days credit, but on the thirty-first day they lost four percent of their profit margin. Early insistence on timely payments resulted in Osborne Computer Corporation always having good accounts receivable. Rarely did "aging" exceed forty-five days.

The major dealer complaint always has to do with excessive competition. Dealers do not want every Larry, Moe, and Curly in the neighborhood selling the current hot product. To allay this gripe, we agreed to control the number of Osborne dealers. In this country it is illegal to grant dealership territories, but a manufacturer can limit the total number of dealerships in any geographic location, which is what Osborne Computer Corporation did.

We also knew that other manufacturers had, from time to time, attempted to control the size of their dealer network, only to be thwarted by unauthorized dealers of every stripe, who obtained product from who-knows-where, then sold it with little or no support.

One early Osborne dealer based in Pittsburgh, Pennsylvania, told me incredulously of a customer who once asked when the dealer would be by to install the customer's Apple II computer. Not remembering this customer, the dealer inquired about the purchase. The customer explained that he had bought the computer from a mail order company in Los Angeles who assured him that any local Apple dealer would be happy to install the computer—without charge, of course.

Unauthorized dealers buy product from renegade, authorized dealers who accept a tiny markup in return for cash on delivery.

To combat unauthorized dealers, Osborne Computer Corporation did not allow dealers to resell product to any other dealer. This policy was enforced by turning seven percent of the dealer margin into a credit applied to the dealer's next purchase. But the credit was given only when we received the computer warranty card. Because the warranty card identified the customer, the dealer, and the product's serial number, unauthorized resales were easily spotted.

Dealer margins were originally determined by a nonenforceable annual volume purchase agreement. The margin was adjusted upward or downward as dealers strayed from their volume commitment in one direction or the other. But this was a clumsy scheme, difficult to manage and fraught with opportunities for dealer discontent. Eventually the scheme was dropped in favor of one that determined margins by the size of individual orders. Osborne Computer Corporation also had a generous cooperative advertising scheme whereby the dealer could spend three percent of his invoice on Osborne product advertising.

Psaris and Hagen put together a formidable dealer network in advance of our first product shipments. The most stellar names in the business were early Osborne dealers: Datel in New York, leading Computerland dealers, Computique in Los Angeles, Macy's, and the Xerox computer store chain, to name a few. In retrospect, however, I believe that the carefully designed dealer program had little if any impact on either product sales or dealers' early stampede to carry the Osborne I. Dealers wanted the product simply because customers walked into their stores asking for it, having read favorable articles about the product or the company in one magazine or another. Certainly Osborne Computer Corporation's generous dealer program did nothing to stem the flow of dealers dropping the product when in 1983 the company lost its momentum and customer following.

The importance of customer perceptions and the inability of dealers to generate product demand will likely be underscored by the IBM PC, with potentially disastrous consequences for dealers.

Dvorak and I both predict that, in the absence of AT&T becoming a significant factor, IBM will curtail the sale of product through computer stores, in which case the computer retailing industry might turn to alternative products. They will be devastated nevertheless, however, because customers will continue to buy IBM personal computers, out of IBM's own showrooms if necessary. Dvorak and I disagree on the significance of AT&T. By the time this book is published, AT&T will probably have announced their own IBM PC compatible microcomputer. If the announcement has not been made, rest assured that it is coming. Dvorak does not believe that AT&T will successfully enter the microcomputer marketplace. I believe they will be very successful—to the extent of forcing IBM to remain in computer stores, if only to keep AT&T out.

Chapter Three THE BALL IS ROLLING

In July of 1981 Osborne Computer Corporation shipped a few demonstration computers to each of its authorized dealers. The delivery schedule had only slipped thirty days during a time when few manufacturers came within six months of their predicted delivery dates. Customers were waiting in line with cash in hand, so dealer confidence in the company boomed when the product arrived on time.

Table 2 compares actual computer shipments during 1981 with the original forecast from the business plan. Taking into account the one-month slip, my original plan proved to be remarkably realistic. As anticipated, we were able to sell everything we could build. For dealers the Osborne I was a "cash cow." They did not have to pay Osborne Computer Corporation (by then generally known as "OCC") for thirty days, yet they received immediate cash from product-hungry customers. It was not until February of 1982 that production could catch up to demand.

Table 2 **A comparison of actual versus forecast Osborne I sales during 1981**

	1981 Unit Sales		
Forecast		*Actual*	
June	200	June	1
July	400	July	242
August	1200	August	612
September	1440	September	856
October	1728	October	1805
November	2074	November	1491
December	2488	December	2045

It is hard to comprehend the euphoria that accompanied those early deliveries. The company had raised only $900,000; yet in the first two months, July and August of 1981, more than $900,000 worth of computers had already been sold. September, the third month of shipments, was the company's first million-dollar month, while orders were all cut to half or less of dealer requests. The company was invincible, and the world had to know.

My own ideas, Davidson's dealmaking, Psaris' marketing and sales programs and dealer plan, and Burdick's public relations—these were the components of the unfolding success. And not one of them would have been accepted, nor any single key player hired by any existing competition before our success. This early triumph provided a tremendous morale boost which in turn seemed to prevent people from questioning future edicts: I was suddenly seen as infallible, in the eyes of employees and investors alike.

Manufacturing difficulties appeared almost instantly, however, leading to Osborne Computer Corporation's first life-threatening crisis.

Following the successful introduction of the Osborne I at the West Coast Computer Faire, Davidson organized the first small production line and started looking for subcontractors. Osborne Computer Corporation intended to assemble and test units only: all components would be bought; all logic boards would be assembled by one of the many companies specializing in this type of work. Thus, working, tested parts would be delivered to us ready to go into our computers.

The bulk of Osborne Computer Corporation's subcontracting business went to Porter Hurt, owner of two interlocking companies: PH Components and Testology. PH Components bought parts; Testology stuffed and tested printed circuit boards, usually using parts purchased by PH Components.

Davidson and Hurt were birds of a feather. Hurt looked like a pork barrel, wore expensive jewelry, and had a fondness for chauffeur-driven, expensive cars. (To me, "pork barrel" seemed to say it all; I've always mused that Hurt might have been a big success in the era of pork-barrel politics.) The relationship between Davidson and Hurt concerned me and other senior management members at Osborne Computer Corporation.

Davidson struck a deal with Hurt in the spring of 1981 that appeared on the surface to be very advantageous to Osborne Computer Corporation. In hindsight, however, I feel that the deal was more advantageous to Porter Hurt.

The contract we had with Testology stated that Osborne Computer Corporation would pay Testology only for delivered, stuffed, and tested printed circuit boards. Each board was to have a one-year guarantee. The problem was that this contract sat on top of another contract between Osborne Computer Corporation and PH Components, Hurt's other company. Under the terms of this second contract, Osborne Computer Corporation had to buy all components used by Testology through PH Components.

Osborne Computer Corporation paid PH Components for components it had purchased, whether or not Testology was actually able to use them in deliverable boards. Components in a logic board cost a good deal more than the labor involved with board stuffing and testing. Osborne Computer Corporation quickly ran into problems in August and September 1981 when Testology was unable make a logic tester work, and consequently were stuffing and testing many boards but delivering very few. We were nevertheless still committed by contract to pay PH Components even for those components that Testology could not make work.

Hurt and Davidson both claim that none of the problems would have occurred if the designs coming from Osborne Computer Corporation's engineering departments had been complete and properly documented. Lee Felsenstein, the original designer of the Osborne I, in fact never finished the documentation for his original creation. Some critics complain that his overly clever design work made the machines difficult to manufacture.

In truth, any seasoned manufacturing executive would have deemed the Osborne I, when first shipped, to be in its preproduction phase, in need of six more months and a couple more prototype development rounds. But there were no manufacturing engineers working for Osborne Computer Corporation at the time, and it was more than a year before anyone really understood how premature the Osborne I had been when first shipped. And yet dealers loved the product.

I, meanwhile, left for the United Kingdom in mid August of 1981 to launch a subsidiary company. Before I left, our bank (Bank of America, Hayward Branch) assured me that the company's financial needs through the end of the year could be easily accommodated. I also received assurances from Davidson that the logic board tester problem was virtually solved. In fact it was not solved for weeks—and Osborne Computer Corporation still owed PH Components for every part in unusable CPU boards sitting at Testology.

There were thousands of boards piling up.

On Friday, September 4, 1981, at 2:00 PM, Greg Belange and Adrianna Crow from the Bank of America came to see me. They were visibly nervous: their mission was to tell me that the bank had changed its mind and would not provide Osborne Computer Corporation with its required loans after all. They faced an alarming increase in accounts payable that was unmatched by compensating computer shipments or by accounts receivable. As far as they were concerned, our company was dead and by Monday morning it would be gone.

Smiling nervously, they assured me that no existing loans would be called before Monday afternoon. The company had the weekend to acquire new equity.

By Monday morning Jack Melchor had pulled a rabbit out of the hat: a $1,600,000 rabbit. He sold some treasury stock at $40 a share, up from $17.39 per share, the price that had been set when the company was raising its first $900,000 in February. The new money came almost entirely from venture capital sources.

The excess printed circuit boards at Testology remained a financial burden to Osborne Computer Corporation for a long time to come since the Osborne I logic design was still undergoing a series of changes. There was at least one board design change each month, and revisions were made upon revisions, which significantly increased the Osborne I cost. And there were other problems as well.

The disk controller board, which had been custom designed to reduce costs, also underwent constant revisions. Also, part of the CP/M operating system that resides on the computer's main logic board contained programming errors (known to programmers, without affection, as "bugs").

The keyboard also had problems. Added to the program corrections, this ultimately required a general product recall in October 1981. Anyone who had previously purchased a computer could take it back to the dealer to have it fixed without charge. Osborne Computer Corporation provided the keyboard fixes, and the dealers donated the service time. This amazing concession on the part of the dealer network was worked out by Psaris and Hagen.

Tom Davidson was not at all in favor of the free fix. "You're givin' away the store!" he complained. "And it's costin' the company money."

I felt that the upgrade policy would be worth more in good will than any extra costs to the company. My appraisal was probably correct. The free upgrade was treated very favorably by the technical press, since it was a new phenomenon for any computer manufacturer to fix problems without charge.

But the product recall was just the tip of a huge iceberg. There were endless design changes that resulted from a lack of real engineering or manufacturing experience in Osborne's management. And we urgently needed such management experience since no company before us had ever attempted to compress so much electronics into such a small space. The interaction between the many components of a microcomputer—the disk drives, display units, power supply, and logic boards—was complex, especially regarding radio frequency emissions and their effect on disk electronics.

Davidson's method of solving problems was to collect Lee Felsenstein, Pat McGuire, and any other active participant and scream at them until they promised to have the problem fixed by the next morning. Fixes were dutifully reported, whether they worked or not. It was beginning to be clear that Davidson was over his head.

All of the early disagreements between Davidson and other members of Osborne management stemmed from a contention that Davidson was hiring woefully inadequate people at almost every level of his organization. Davidson, in turn, felt that Psaris and I were hiring "incompetent losers." One of few people hired by Davidson who I liked was Bob Lemon, the production manager.

But good managers or bad, when fully analyzed the Osborne I problems stemmed from nonexistent quality control. The following memo from me to Davidson exemplifies the dispute that was brewing:

November 19, 1981

TO: Tom Davidson

cc: Curtis Jones
Georgette Psaris
Fred Osowick

FR: Adam Osborne

SUBJ: Quality Control

I wish to commend your quality control department for the egalitarian approach they take toward doing a crummy job. Not only do our customers have to suffer for the lack of proper product inspection, I do too.

I brought to your attention the fact that my OSBORNE I, when upgraded, was returned to me with velcro on the power receptacle cover positioned so that it could do no good. In addition, I was given one side catch that constantly slips open, and a strip on the bottom that would not stay attached to the case.

It is necessary that we check product for physical as well as electronic integrity.

The Osborne I actually may have had some fundamental design problems, but they were masked by the sloppy quality-control standards. The most basic design problem, one that haunted every portable computer manufacturer, was the effect that radio noise from the display had on the disk drives. Unless fully suppressed, this noise distorted signals picked off microscopic magnetic zones on the diskette surface.

To alleviate the engineering overload (and to circumvent Davidson), I turned over new product development to outside consultants. Fred Coury and Curt Ingraham together started work on new products in late 1981, leaving our internal staff to develop the Osborne I upgrades.

The first model had only a fifty-two-column display on a diminutive five-inch screen. The disk drives were single density, so a diskette could only hold about 100,000 characters. A double density upgrade would double the disk storage capacity. The eighty-column upgrade would allow eighty characters per line to be displayed. Initially Osborne Computer Corporation had planned to start shipping double density upgrades by December 1981 and eighty-column upgrades shortly thereafter.

But it was October of 1982 before the double density option was available, while the eighty-column upgrade was not introduced until January of 1983. These were Osborne's first major delays. They hurt the company's credibility because the press had already quoted our claims that these upgrades would be ready before the end of 1981.

Euphoria has a nasty habit of stumbling on reality.

The most pressing Osborne I improvement remained the need for an injection molded case. By late 1981 parameters of Osborne I had settled down sufficiently for work on this new case to begin. Tom Davidson was at that time in favor of moving to a nine-inch monitor, but I was so concerned about the endless engineering snafus that I insisted on keeping the five-inch screen to avoid additional delays from new elements. Also, the nine-inch screen would give off even stronger radio frequency signals, making it even harder for the disk drives to work reliably. It was July of 1982 before injection molded cases were ready—almost two months after the planned introduction date.

Should the company have switched from the five-inch monitor to a nine-inch monitor when making the case change?

There is no doubt the answer is yes—*if* the disk drive reliability problems could have been solved in time, and *if* the plastic case design changes could have been implemented with no further delays. The disk drive probelms weren't solved until June of 1982.

Yet through the fall of 1981, it seemed as if nothing could hurt sales. The engineering problems and management disputes that swirled around Tom Davidson were obscured by the avalanche of orders resulting from a hugely successful advertising campaign.

Because of its success, Osborne Computer Corporation soon outgrew its manufacturing space. By the end of 1981 manufacturing had moved into a new building a block away from the original headquarters. In this building Tom Davidson put together a manufacturing facility that would be able to meet the demand.

But even while expanding its manufacturing facilities, the senior managers agreed that manufacturing should be taken offshore as soon as possible. Davidson traveled to Japan, Taiwan, and Hong Kong to locate potential manufacturing sites. He also needed to negotiate for the purchase of low-cost parts. He was generally successful in both endeavors. He found a number of viable offshore manufacturers for the Osborne I, but the product did not stabilize enough to give it to a contract manufacturer until 1982, and by then it was obsolete.

One of the more amazing Davidson stories occurred during his first Far East trip when he visited a major Japanese semiconductor manufacturer. Following the Japanese ritual exchange of business cards, Tom mimed an atomic bomb explosion before his startled hosts to make the point that he was in Japan fighting for really low prices.

While Davidson was the source of amazing stories abroad, Ben Counter kept right on producing surprises at home.

One example arose in the fall of 1981, when Barbara Burdick noticed that Ben Counter's accounts receivable clerk was donating her time to other office personnel seeking help. Barbara was curious.

"Why isn't Ben keeping you busy?" she inquired.

"Oh," the clerk replied, "Ben stopped processing accounts receivable a couple of weeks ago."

"Stopped . . . processing . . . accounts receivable?" Barbara asked, not quite sure she had heard correctly.

"That's right," the clerk replied. "The new data processing manager wiped out all the data files so the computer won't process receivables any more."

Barbara paid Ben a visit.

"I understand you aren't processing any receivables," she noted casually, "or sending out any invoices."

"The computer has been down. It isn't processing anything correctly," Ben replied apologetically.

"What . . . are you doing about it?" Barbara asked.

"I don't know what to do yet," Ben replied.

"Have you told Adam?" Barbara asked.

"Oh no!" Ben replied, a look of horror crossing his generally emotionless face.

"I think you should tell Adam," Barbara replied, "before he finds out. I think Adam would like to know that no one has been billed in two weeks."

Ben did tell me what had happened. Invoicing resumed immediately, with the work being done by hand until the data processing files could be reconstructed.

On another occasion Ben admitted with a slightly crestfallen expression that he had forgotten a half-million-dollar accounts payable item. He had forgotten it because the amount was almost identical to another payable falling due at approximately the same time.

So the company's first major executive recruitment campaign set about finding a vice president of finance. When this became generally known, Ben Counter came to see me. He wanted to explain that, in his opinion, he had capabilities far exceeding anything that he had been asked to do and should be given the new spot. He wasn't.

Jim Ottinger was given the job. Ottinger came from Memorex and was recommended by Melchor. He was the first Osborne executive who looked his part. The rest of the company had the loose Berkeley style, but Jim was a three-piece-suiter. He would eventually be part of what some employees would call, in disgust, the new "button-down management."

Until the end of 1981 all personnel administration had been handled by Marlene Tanner, my administrative assistant. Clearly, the company had reached the point where, with more than fifty employees, a professional Human Resources Department was badly needed. Jeff Boynton was hired to handle this task.

Boynton is a robust-looking professional with a preference for doing things by the book. Despite a military background, he remained sufficiently flexible to cope with the unusual people and surroundings that he found at Osborne Computer Corporation. His first major assignment, which he attacked with gusto, was to organize the 1981 company Christmas party. It was held on a chartered ferry boat that cruised a fog-bound, storm-battered San Francisco Bay. But rain and fog or not, there was probably no other time when the company mood was more optimistic and free of war wounds. The company had its share of problems, but they were buried under an avalanche of orders.

Table 3 shows the financial results reported for the year ending November 1981.

Table 3 **Income statement, year end November 28, 1981.**

Osborne Computer Corporation
Consolidated Statement of Operations
and Accumulated Deficit
Year End November 28, 1981

Net sales		$5,761,000
Costs and expenses:		
Cost of sales	$3,878,000	
Marketing	960,000	
Research, development and initial production	1,282,000	
General and administrative	832,000	
Interest, net	91,000	7,043,000
Net loss		(1,282,000)
Accumulated deficit, at November 29, 1980		(38,000)
Accumulated deficit, at November 28, 1981		$(1,320,000)

A QUESTION OF INTERNATIONAL SALES

In addition to establishing a strong domestic dealer network, Osborne Computer Corporation intended to start exporting its computer as quickly as possible.

Anyone coming late into the microcomputer market should pay close attention to exports. Europe runs about a year behind the United States, and Canada runs roughly six months behind us. Selling in Europe is therefore akin to having started in the USA a year earlier.

My plan was to establish subsidiary companies in countries with large sales potential, relying on distributors to handle the rest of the international market.

Subsidiary companies were planned for the United Kingdom, Germany, and Australia. The company used distributors in France and Italy. Although France was a country with a large sales potential, the French inferiority complex when confronted with anything Anglo or American demands that one sneak product into that country through a French distributor, disguising the product's non-French origins whenever possible.

Any American microcomputer company with a hot product must establish its own European market—and quickly—otherwise the "gray market" will take over. In between beating their chests and protesting their integrity, some small percentage of American dealers respond to cash waved under their noses by selling anything to anyone. The cash-wavers are a small group of aggressive European hucksters who dump product all over Europe without addressing the inconvenience of customer support. This problem emerged very quickly. In our case indignant customers started writing and calling from all over Europe before the end of 1981. They were unimpressed with protestations that they comprised an unanticipated problem with which we could not cope. They had a machine, they wanted support, and that was that. Had we done nothing, the Osborne I would have developed a bad reputation, making later European penetration impossible.

I knew the "gray market" would be a problem and so I made my first trip to Europe in June of 1981, before the first Osborne I had been shipped. Few Americans really understand that Europe is a collection of very different countries, most of which are quite small. And to sell well in Europe, a low-cost computer such as the Osborne I must be customized from country to country. In the United Kingdom the change was small: one key showing the English pound sign. But through the rest of

Europe, keyboard modifications were more extensive and displays had to be translated into a variety of languages.

In an amazing demonstration of nationalism, European countries invariably adopted keyboards that differed slightly from one to another. Some European countries (notably Scandinavia) have additional letters in their alphabets that necessitate different keyboards, but why should Norway and Sweden adopt keyboards with just one different key location? Germany moves the "z" key. The French have a totally different AZERTY keyboard, which they then complicate by also having a French variation of the standard QWERTY key layout. Switzerland has no less than five standard keyboards.

The groundwork was laid for Osborne Computer Corporation's international organization in the fall of 1981. Operations came together early in 1982, first headed by Mike McCullough, who joined the company in mid-1981 as director of domestic marketing, reporting to Georgette Psaris. McCullough has a very un-American talent: he speaks six languages. Coming from Intel, he brought with him considerable knowledge of the semiconductor industry, together with excellent international contacts. McCullough seemed ideally suited to international operations.

When transferred to the International Department, McCullough immediately began an aggressive recruitment campaign. First he hired Dave Miller away from Intel.

Dave provided Osborne with a strong technical background. Also, because he spent part of his youth in Europe, he had developed an excellent international perspective. He was given the responsibility for generating European versions of the Osborne I computer, including customized keyboards and local language displays.

Although McCullough was a talented salesman, he wasn't necessarily a talented manager. Al Stone was hired to provide this balance. Both men can be described as high-energy go-getters. Unfortunately, it appeared that the company had picked two individuals who didn't get along with each other. In April of 1982 it was necessary to get Ron Brown to supervise both men. Brown was hired as vice president for international operations.

McCullough recruited Sepp Hatzl to become president of Osborne GMBH in Germany. Sepp, an energetic, full-bearded Austrian, established Osborne's German head office in Munich. He proceeded with Germanic efficiency to close down the "gray market" for unauthorized Osborne I's in Germany by quickly introducing a German keyboard and display. Sepp Hatzl's principal adversary was Volbus, a Berlin-based mail-order outfit that had probably sold 500 Osborne I's by mid-1982. Although this number could never be verified, the trail of disgruntled owners with nowhere to turn for service or support quickly sensitized Sepp to the dangers posed by companies such as Volbus.

In Spain, Mike McCullough recruited Investronica to act as Osborne's distributor. This company is a subsidiary of one of Spain's largest corporations. Investronica already represented Sinclair and later was appointed distributor for IBM personal computers. Selling microcomputers through the El Cortez Ingles store chain, Investronica quickly positioned the Osborne I among the leaders in the Spanish microcomputer market.

In early 1982 portable computers were still a novelty throughout Europe. Yet as I traveled from country to country with a portable computer at the end of my arm, very few customs officials gave this novelty a second glance . . . until I reached Spain. At the Madrid airport I received my first hostile reception. It came from customs officials who did not know what to make of the strange device fancifully being described as a "computer." Computers occupied entire rooms, not small suitcases. Was it a bomb, an espionage device, a weird radio? The customs officials would have none of it and were determined to hold the strange electronic contraption until I departed. Only vigorous intercession on the part of my Spanish hosts managed to convince customs officials that the microcomputer was indeed harmless and would be leaving the country with its owner in a few days.

Within three days I struck a deal with Investronica, who immediately started working on Spanish documentation for a Spanish Osborne I. Meanwhile Investronica negotiated with the well-known Spanish brandy manufacturer of the same name to ensure that Osborne microcomputers could be sold simultaneously with Osborne brandy.

In Belgium, Osborne products were distributed by the Drion Organization which also handled Sinclair products. Belgium is a small country with a remarkably large banking and insurance industry; consequently the Drions were quite successful selling Osborne products.

Nowhere was Osborne more successful in its choice of distributors than in Scandinavia. Nord Sales represented Osborne in Norway. Rolf Carrick, the ex-Apple distributor, was appointed in Sweden to distribute Osborne computers. In Denmark the choice was Formula Micro run by Bent Petersen, and in Finland, Komdel Oy, run by Martti Laine.

Considering the size of the country, no distributor in the world was as successful as Knut Johansson and Nord Sales in Norway. Knut sold more computers in Norway than any other distributor in any other country in Europe, with the exception of Britain and Germany. For a while Knut's Norwegian sales were outstripping Apple and IBM combined. Finland, likewise, was an outstanding success. Sales quickly rose to an average of 50–100 microcomputers per month, which for a country the size of Finland is outstanding.

In Denmark the industrious Danes even went so far as to customize the Osborne I for the Faeroe Islanders whose forty thousand inhabitants have their own language and alphabet.

But there were also spectacular failures in Europe. In France Mike McCullough appointed Tekelec as the primary distributor. Tekelec is a large company that distributes electronic components. As the French representative for Altos, their reported shipments of Altos computers must have accounted for a significant percentage of Altos' worldwide business. But Altos sold primarily to an industrial customer base. Osborne was looking for retail outlets. Tekelec did poorly for Osborne.

In France Osborne Computer Corporation also attempted to distribute product through the French Rank Xerox Organization, but with little success. By mid-1983 approximately one thousand Osborne I's had been sold in France, mostly by France's few Computerland stores. In 1983 Bernard Maniglier started a French company to distribute Osborne I computers, but his efforts were thwarted by the company's bankruptcy.

In Italy, IRET was likewise unable to sell many Osborne I's. Originally the Apple distributor, IRET's relations with Apple had become quite strained and they were anxious to move on. Their efforts on behalf of Osborne were nonetheless unsuccessful, since they were slow at introducing the Italian version of the Osborne I. Moreover, in the absence of any Italian computer retail market, IRET had established a network of small computer consulting groups; but after investing so much time and effort in Apple programs, they were not interested in switching to another brand of microcomputer.

Of all the foreign countries entered, Osborne Computer Corporation was most successful in the United Kingdom, where the microcomputer market is similar to the United States, also having a large number of computer stores. Throughout Europe the product assortment tends to run approximately twelve months behind the USA. As a result, there are still a large number of unique microcomputers selling in the UK, in sharp contrast to the standardization trend already far advanced in the USA. Also, people in the UK in general have less disposable income. They buy microcomputers to operate small businesses rather than for personal use. Thus they extend the capabilities of simple machines with extreme ingenuity, performing tasks that to an American would appear improbable at best. The Sinclair ZX81, for example, is used to handle payroll and accounting functions in very small UK companies.

The Osborne I fit into the UK market very well. It provided low-cost computing which appealed to the thrifty British buyer. Microcomputers always cost more in the UK than the USA, but the Osborne I price difference was, relatively speaking, very small since Osborne Computer Corporation distributed directly. An American microcomputer typically costs twice as much in the UK as it does in the USA, but the Osborne I costs approximately forty percent more in the UK, much of which represents freight, taxes, and duty.

Mike Healey, the president of the Osborne UK subsidiary, started selling Osborne I's in February of 1982. By early 1983 he was selling more than five hundred microcomputers per month. By the summer of that year, while the parent company was going bankrupt, Healey was fighting for first place among UK microcomputers selling between 1,000 and 2,000 pounds sterling.

Osborne Computer Corporation also did very well in Australia and South Africa. In Australia, under the direction of Richard Graham, the company averaged roughly two hundred microcomputers per month, giving Osborne Computer Corporation a significant market share in that country.

Overall, Osborne Computer Corporation's policy had been to keep costs low in foreign countries by establishing a directly owned subsidiary in any country that had a sufficient volume potential. Nonexclusive distributors were appointed elsewhere.

If a distributor did a good job, he was allowed to operate exclusively, but the threat of competition was always present. Only in Spain did Osborne Computer Corporation sign an exclusive distributorship, and then only because laws peculiar to that country made it necessary.

It is very dangerous for small companies to sign exclusive distributorships in Europe since the natural self-interests of the distributor and the manufacturer are very different. The manufacturer wants the distributor to sell a lot of product for a small margin. The distributor can make just as much money in the absence of competition by selling a little product for a very large markup. In Europe, Osborne made a point of simultaneously dealing both with a distributor and with Computerland International, whose stores could buy directly from the central Computerland operation or from the local national Osborne distributor.

In France, at one extreme, Computerland stores represented the bulk of Osborne sales. In Norway, at the other extreme, Computerland was barely able to function at all, faced with the stiff competition provided by Nord Sales.

The international market was very important to Osborne Computer Corporation, accounting for approximately twenty-five percent of total sales during the months of hypergrowth. The export market is a difficult arena for small American manufacturers, but it is also very rewarding. But the problem an American company faces if they avoid the European market is that domestic success breeds foreign trouble. Successful American products reach Europe anyway; in the absence of support, this can generate expensive chaos.

Chapter Four CRISIS TIME

In December 1981, Jim Ottinger was given the task of finding a good financial reporting and control system for Osborne Computer Corporation using computer equipment that could handle the task. Ben Counter used an Altos microcomputer system, but it didn't work. I had selected the Altos microcomputer system myself; since we were a microcomputer company, I felt we should use micros whenever possible. It turned out to be wasted idealism. A larger system was still sorely needed.

It was April of 1982 before a reasonable semblance of a financial reporting system was installed, due largely to the efforts of Mike Anthofer, a remarkably talented individual hired by Jim Ottinger to do the work while Ottinger managed. I've always thought of Anthofer as one of those gifted financial professionals who can see sufficiently beyond the numbers to laugh at them.

Meanwhile, the company's financial reporting was approximate at best. I prepared the 1982 budget, with Barbara Burdick's assistance, using an Osborne I and SuperCalc.

The company's failure to quickly implement an adequate financial control system made market planning very difficult. To make matters worse, each department was developing its own numbers by hand. Departments would be told they were over budget or out of money for no apparent reason, and it was mid-summer before adequate controls were in place.

Meanwhile, Fred Osowick had been hired in the latter part of 1981 to head the service organization, reporting to Georgette Psaris. Fred is a touch service professional. In order to take the abuse that comes with the job, Fred freely admitted that a good service manager needs a streak of masochism in him—but Fred's masochistic tendencies were not extreme enough to tolerate Tom Davidson. He and Tom did not get along.

In early January of 1982, Psaris came to see me. "Fred Osowick has raised a red flag," she said. "There has been an alarming increase in Osborne I's being reported by dealers 'dead on arrival'." (This meant units were found to be defective when received.)

I immediately spoke to Tom Davidson who was convinced that dealers were overcommitted and simply wanted to "get out from under."

"There aren't no quality control problems," he contended. "Who'd suffer more than me if the problem was real? Sure, an occasional batch of computers go out with some machines that don't work, but that'll happen anywhere!"

For some time I had been nervous about just such an eventuality. So I had kept my own record of product reliability, keeping a daily score of shipments, in-house yields, and dealer returns. Table 4 summarizes the statistics I recorded for December 1981 and January 1982. Following a surge of problems in November, the situation had improved slightly in December, only to return with a vengeance in January. Very few units that dealers sold were returned by customers. It was the dealers themselves who were returning unsold computers.

Table 4 **Manufacturing, shipping and returns of Osborne I computers for November, December 1981 and January 1982.**

Date	*Built*	*Shipped*	*Customer Returns to Dealer*	*Dealer Returns to Factory*
November Total	988	1392	82	326
December 1	54	85	2	25
2	57	104	4	21
3	80	110	2	19
4	88	118	1	10
5	0	0	0	0
6	0	0	0	0
7	124	155	4	13
8	70	115	9	13
9	87	141	0	23
10	78	122	3	17
11	77	121	2	16
12	0	0	0	0
13	0	0	0	0
14	102	127	2	31

Crisis Time

Date	*Built*	*Shipped*	*Customer Returns to Dealer*	*Dealer Returns to Factory*
15	96	116	10	28
16	104	134	0	10
17	91	136	2	37
18	110	140	4	29
19	0	0	0	0
20	0	0	0	0
21	175	167	3	32
22	96	124	1	12
23	72	117	2	25
December Total	1561	2132	51	361
January 1	0	0	0	0
2	0	0	0	0
3	0	0	0	0
4	92	124	4	50
5	101	148	5	80
6	103	130	1	30
7	93	149	12	57
8	106	130	0	21
9	0	0	0	0
10	0	0	0	0
11	141	101	1	29
12	131	52	0	37
13	94	215	1	34
14	122	111	6	14
15	132	111	10	32
16	0	0	0	0
17	0	0	0	0
18	162	166	3	23
19	140	122	6	41
20	142	315	1	41
21	130	168	1	29
22	120	155	1	13
23	0	0	0	0
24	0	0	0	0
25	0	0	2	12
January Total	1809	2197	54	543

Note 1: The company was closed from December 24 until January 4.
Note 2: For accounting purposes the end of January was January 25.

Fred Osowick continued to scream warnings. Tom Davidson first denied the accuracy of the data: when it was confirmed he attributed the problem to a single freak shipment. But the facts were as stark as they were simple: the endless series of ill-defined solutions to unanalyzed problems had finally caught up with us.

A variety of simplistic causes for the problems were trotted out, including dirty disk duplicators and poor quality diskettes, but by early February dealers were canceling orders faster than they were placing them. Computer Mart of New Orleans was the curious single exception; they continued ordering amazingly high volumes. This revealed them as the principal conduit for Osborne I computers that had appeared all over Europe within weeks of the first domestic product shipments. Being unsupported, these European machines caused problems. So despite the problems at home, I spent the last week of January 1982 in Great Britain and France, hurrying along my European operations. In France Barbara and I were photographed by *Fortune* magazine walking arm-in-arm down the Champs Elysées. Would that the situation had been as idyllic as that photograph suggested!

While I was gone Dan Brown, one of the company's key programmers, stopped by to see Georgette Psaris. He knew what "the real problem" was, he told Georgette. Some four months earlier he had told Lee Felsenstein about a nasty little bug in the Osborne I's "BIOS," a piece of the operating system program that sits in a chip on the computer board.

One of many marathon round-the-clock sessions began. Fred Osowick organized "tiger teams" that fanned out around the country visiting dealers and fixing computers in the dealers' own stores. Dan Brown and Roger Chapman meanwhile fixed the program bug that Dan had found. By the middle of February the problem was resolved. The rampant enthusiasm in every quarter of the company would not allow any unsolved problem to exist. There was a solution, and the solution had to be found. It was that simple.

Once the magnitude of the January crisis became apparent, I promoted Ed Richter to vice president of engineering and moved him out from under Tom Davidson's control. Richter had recently been hired as director of engineering. He immediately identified a more fundamental disk drive probelm, one that came with being a pioneer. We were cramming two disk drives into one small box, close to a power supply and a video display tube, both of which have a nasty habit of emitting radio noise that confuses disk-drive read mechanisms. So in early April product shipments were again stopped while Ed figured out a "final" fix for this problem.

The effect of these disruptions are shown in Table 5, which compares product shipments between January and June of 1982 with both the originally conceived plan and the budget prepared at the end of 1982. Tables 6 and 7 show how the company's financial performance suffered during the quarters ending in February and May of 1982 as a consequence of the February crisis.

Table 5 **A comparison of actual Osborne I unit sales with original forecast and 1982 medium-range plan for January through June, 1982.**

Month	*Original 1981 Business Plan*[1]	*1982 Budget Numbers*[2]	*Actual*[3]
January	2687	3000	2000
February	2902	3950	3800
March	3135	4700	2600
April	3385	6200	1900
May	3656	7900	2000
June	3949	10000	2750

[1]Note: "1981 Plan" is the number of units specified for shipment in the original business plan (see Table 1).
[2]Note: "1982 Budget" represents the revised numbers for the same months, prepared in late 1981 as part of the 1982 budget.
[3]Note: "Actual" represents the actual number of units shipped for the same month.

During the 1982 quality control crisis, Bob Marsh showed up in March of that year with a finished, working, double density upgrade board for the Osborne I. Marsh, a long-time associate of Lee Felsenstein, had been a principal at Processor Technology, a microcomputer manufacturer that enjoyed brief prominence in the late seventies. Richter reported that the Marsh board was theoretically flawed and its implementation would cause problems. He recommended staying with the double density board then being readied in-house for release in late April. But no one could present any evidence of real problems with the Marsh board, and Felsenstein stuck by the design. I sided with Richter. Having become very preoccupied with quality and reliability, I favored the Richter report over objections from Marsh and Felsenstein. The in-house double density board was subsequently shown to be flawed. It would be nearly nine months before the promised double density upgrade actually appeared. And for all that time the Marsh board worked perfectly.

The dust settled, as it invariably does, and a small number of Osborne I's were shipped during May 1982. But units with the new injection molded case were due in June. In anticipation of this, the company deliberately restricted shipments. Dealers' shelves had to be empty when the new, more attractive units arrived, at which time any remaining supply of the old brown case units would become problem merchandise.

Table 6 **Income statement quarter end February 27, 1982.**

	Quarter End February 27, 1982 (in thousands, except per-share amounts)
Net sales	$8,702
Cost of sales	6,618
Gross profit	2,084
Selling, general, and administrative expenses	2,085
Research and development	154
Interest expense	115
Income (loss) before income taxes	(270)
Provision for income taxes	—
Net income (loss)	$(270)
Earnings (loss) per common and common equivalent share	(.11)

Under Georgette Psaris' expert guidance, the transition from the old case to the new case units went very smoothly. Psaris, working with Lynn Hagen and two recent additions, Fred and Pete Brown, developed a plan to keep dealers happy. Fred, a born salesman, had been hired as director of national accounts. Later he became director and then vice president of sales. Pete headed up the customer support group. Between them they instituted a policy of inventory balancing. Dealers were encouraged to return computers on the slightest hint of overstocking. The returned goods were then reshipped to dealers with a critical need for product. By the time new case units were shipped, dealers were desperate for product, even though they were entering the slow summer season, a time of year when dealers are usually overloaded with unsellable goods.

It was July 1982 before the company finally caught up with dealer demand again. But the slowdown in product shipment caused the second major cash crisis, which Jack Melchor solved by raising $10 million in new venture capital at the equivalent of $150 per share. He raised this money within thirty days after Jim Ottinger informed the Board that more equity was needed.

Table 7 **Income statement quarter end May 29, 1982.**

	Quarter End May 29, 1982 (in thousands, except per-share amounts)
Net sales	$10,015
Cost of sales	8,466
Gross profit	1,549
Selling, general, and administrative expenses	2,369
Research and development	176
Interest expense	343
Income (loss) before income taxes	(1,339)
Provision for income taxes	—
Net income (loss)	$(1,339)
Earnings (loss) per common and common equivalent share	(.53)

These funds were raised by issuing Series A preferred shares. For direct comparisons with stock prices given in later chapters, Osborne stock was subsequently split so that ten new shares were issued for each old share. Thus, the adjusted Series A preferred share price was equivalent to $15 per new share.

The crisis faced by Osborne Computer Corporation in the first half of

1982 was severe—as severe as the crisis that precipitated the company's bankruptcy a year later. In 1982 the company had one product that for almost two months could not be shipped because of engineering problems. That product was about to be replaced by the newer double density model—hardly a backdrop that would generate sales, or confidence in the company.

But this is where the company shone. Osborne Computer Corporation was driven by the will of its employees: they believed—we all did. We had already proven once that miracles were possible. Now we simply had to prove it again. The will to succeed became a self-fulfilling prophecy because it translated into pragmatic action. Problems were solved quickly and money was raised without delay, all against an ongoing backdrop of first class public relations.

The key was a wave of highly positive publicity backed by programs aimed at maintaining customer satisfaction. In February 1982 articles appeared simultaneously in *Business Week* and *Fortune* magazines causing a stampede of customers into computer stores. Bewildered managers found themselves canceling orders because of reliability problems at the beginning of the month, then reordering by the middle of the month to meet customer demand.

Fred Osowick's field service group, meanwhile, responded quickly to every dealer complaint; Pete Brown's customer support organization took good care of end-users. The cost was high but customers remained satisfied.

Just by chance, while the company was struggling to maintain momentum and revive sales to the high levels of the previous months, an important survey was taken. During February of 1982, Future Computing, Portia Isaacson's well-known consulting group, surveyed computer store sell-through. It reported Osborne I's selling at a rate of six to eight computers per store per month—a number exceeded only by Apple and IBM. This fact was reported widely by the technical press.

Ironically, the news was received within the company as a humorous irony. Had Portia conducted her survey a month earlier, she would have reported Osborne I's selling in the high teens, a number comparable to Apple or IBM.

From a marketing viewpoint two important lessons were learned during Osborne's crisis of early 1982:

1) Momentum feeds on itself, and
2) Positive customer perceptions create momentum.

Perhaps the more important lesson learned at this time was the importance of customer perceptions. A successful advertising and public relations campaign maintained a high demand for the product. Because of proper support there was no discernible increase in customer disaffection with a defective product, so long as the customer knew it would be fixed. They kept walking into computer stores asking for Osbornes, thereby passing on to the dealer the perception of the Osborne I as the computer to carry.

So long as the momentum of sales was maintained, optimistic sales projections could be both made and met. Had there been any interruption in the strong marketing program or positive public relations campaign, the ranks of new customers would immediately have thinned and the momentum would have been lost. Then every sales projection would have been wrong.

This is precisely what happened exactly a year later, in the absence of any marketing program and with a dwindling public relations campaign.

So while the outside world thought everything was rosy, the company was still in turmoil. By March of 1982 it was clear to everyone that senior management was in need of change. Tom Davidson was the target.

Davidson argued that the recession of 1981 had caused the February downturn. Product reliability, according to Tom, had nothing to do with the problem. He complained bitterly that if he had been put in charge of sales and marketing, the February downturn wouldn't have occurred.

Davidson's last accomplishment was to establish Osborne Computer Corporation's second manufacturing facility south of New Brunswick, New Jersey. This facility would have made more sense if the company had not encountered manufacturing problems.

The idea was that another facility could offer East Coast dealers local manufacturing and support, together with reduced freight cost. These advantages would offset the extra expense of operating two manufacturing plants

In early April of 1982, Tom was encouraged to take his vacation so that manufacturing could be reorganized in his absence. A search began immediately for a vice president of operations and for a director of quality assurance. These two spots were filled, respectively, by George Carr, who came from Atari, and by Dan Costa, who came from National Semiconductor via Jerry Anderson's company, Two Pi. Ron Brown also joined the company at this time as vice president in charge of international operations. Like Jim Ottinger, these senior managers fit the industry mold. They looked like businessmen. Osborne Computer Corporation was becoming respectable.

In retrospect I think that it would have been in the company's best interest to fire Davidson at the beginning of April. Instead, when Davidson returned from vacation he was made vice chairman of the Board and put in charge of negotiating contracts with vendors—his forte.

Until George Carr and Dan Costa were hired, I took personal charge of manufacturing and quality assurance, aided by Bob Lemon and Ed Richter. The people who had manned Tom Davidson's quality assurance department were removed. In the absence of any quality assurance program, I appealed directly to the assemblers on the shop floor. I called a meeting and told everyone just how grave the problem was. I told the assemblers that there was no one to check their work. For the next two months product reliability started and ended with them. My message was very simple: "If you wouldn't buy it, then don't pass it."

I was placing the responsibility for quality back on the workers, a technique common to Silicon Valley operations. They responded magnificently. There was an immediate and marked improvement in product quality. The assembly line workers had tasted authority. They could talk knowing that management would listen. If they complained about product quality, their voices were heard. Until Osborne's last days they remained the toughest enforcers of quality within the company.

It was also at this time that I started my own version of quality circles.

Since I was still working part-time, I made a habit of walking around the manufacturing assembly lines and the offices talking to people at random about what they were doing. Thus, I was able to keep in fast and close touch with day-to-day events.

But a reality quickly became apparent: most of the company's problems were being detected first among the rank and file. Reports that ultimately filtered up to the executive suite were frequently muted, even distorted. The vested self-interests behind many of the distortions were quite transparent. Worse, there were occasional indications of retribution after an employee had talked critically to me while I made my rounds.

Five quality circles were established, each with five members. Each quality circle was charged with addressing a specific area of company activity or concern, such as employee morale, shipping and receiving, and quality assurance. The company's nonsupervisory personnel were divided into five groups by employee function, and from each group one employee was appointed to each quality circle.

Appointments were made from randomly drawn lists. Each month one employee dropped out of each quality circle. The person was replaced by the employee at the top of his or her group's list. If the selected employee declined the appointment, the employee's name went to the bottom of the list and the next name on the list was drawn. Thus, once appointed, each employee spent five months on a quality circle.

Quality circles each met twice a month to discuss anything they chose, shielded by an absolute anti-retribution guarantee. Their meetings were summarized in a memo to me. I responded personally to each memo, obtaining additional responses from other managers when necessary.

The major tangible achievement of the quality circles was identifying some very serious employee discontent at the New Jersey facility. For example, the manager of this facility had given orders that manufacturing personnel (who reported to him) should avoid all contact with marketing employees who shared space in the building but reported to Psaris. This edict applied to working hours as well as social contact outside the plant. Additionally, the quality circles provided a constant stream of suggestions for improving efficiency and employee morale.

Because of my one-on-one contacts with employees, and the power of the quality circles, the fervor among the rank and file bordered on a populist movement. But the quality circles were not nearly so well received within the ranks of management. Many managers thought their authority was being undermined. The resistance to the quality circle program grew to a point where I had to recognize my managers' objections. So Jeff Boynton modified the quality circle program to make it more conventional. When Bob Jaunich arrived, the entire program was discontinued.

It was in the midst of this turmoil, in May 1982, that I finally started working full-time for Osborne Computer Corporation. I also started looking for Tom's replacement. It was a search that would end almost nine months later when Robert Jaunich was hired in January of 1983.

Chapter Five BOOM TIMES

The summer of 1982 was a rerun of the previous year—in living color. Everything was ten times as big and ten times as successful. Osborne Computer Corporation rolled through the summer of 1982 with a happy domestic dealer network smiling at the smooth transition from brown case (vacuum-formed) to blue case (injection-molded) Osborne I computers. While the rest of the computer industry bemoaned the slow summer, Osborne's sales had its first $10 million month that August. We had every reason to be optimistic. Underwriters started knocking at the door begging us to consider a public stock offering, but there was very little enthusiasm for such a move.

I felt that a public offering was premature, given the uncertainty and consequent turmoil caused by the company's rapid growth. The Board of Directors also showed little enthusiasm for a public offering, fresh as they were from the problems of the spring.

September of 1982 saw the departure of Tom Davidson.

Along with others, I had been suspicious of Davidson's relationship with Porter Hurt, although no specific evidence of improprieties surfaced until late 1982, after Davidson's resignation had been forced. We felt Davidson had helped Hurt get into competition with Osborne by bringing the Access Matrix computer to his attention. The designer of the Access Matrix had contacted Tom Davidson in February of 1982 to inquire if Osborne would be interested in his product. I believe that Davidson took the product to Porter Hurt, unbeknownst to anyone else at Osborne Computer Corporation.

I discovered that Davidson invited at least one potential vendor to Hayward; then, instead of discussing Osborne's buying needs, he took the vendor to Porter Hurt to see what business the vendor might have for PH Components or Testology. Juggi Tandon of Tandon Magnetics reports receiving this treatment.

In August of 1982 Davidson was sent to Taiwan to negotiate with a Taiwanese firm for the manufacture of injection-molded plastic cases for new product use.

In early September, after Davidson had returned from Taiwan, he gave an extraordinary interview to a couple of Italian journalists representing one of Italy's leading microcomputer magazines. The interview occurred in Davidson's plush home. The reporters wanted Davidson's views on future trends in the microcomputer industry; but instead, Davidson launched into a diatribe on the contribution he had made to Osborne Computer Corporation and how unrecognized his efforts had been. He particularly criticized me for having grabbed all the headlines and glory. The entire interview was recorded by the startled Italian journalists who ran straight to the company with their tale of our disloyal employee. On the tape Davidson had mentioned something about "doing it all by himself the next time."

At the same time two other interesting pieces of information reached me. Stan Wilkendorf, who had represented Osborne Computer Corporation in Hong Kong, reported that the Taiwanese case manufacturer selected by Tom was also building the Access Matrix's plastic case for Porter Hurt. In addition, Jerry Pournelle, the well-known science fiction author and microcomputer columnist, called me to find out if I knew the details of either Porter Hurt's involvement with Access Matrix, or Davidson's supposed participation in the venture. Pournelle had gotten his information from Bill Godbout, a competitor of Porter Hurt turned microcomputer manufacturer himself.

The picture appeared clear to me: Tom Davidson was working with Porter Hurt to develop a competing product.

Osborne Computer Corporation was in an extremely vulnerable position since Porter Hurt, still the only source for Osborne electronics boards, could at any time have closed the company down by refusing to supply boards.

Faced by this potentially disastrous situation, the company waited a few days until Davidson would be in Los Angeles with Jim Ottinger, Georgette Psaris, and myself attending an awards celebration at which Osborne Computer Corporation was to be given an industrial achievement award.

Davidson had a wonderful time in Los Angeles. He hired himself a Cadillac limousine with chauffeur; no taxi or rental car would do. Meanwhile we all knew the ax was about to fall, and we probably all could have won Oscars for our acting. We betrayed nothing for fear that Davidson might remove incriminating evidence from his office if he got wind of what was about to happen.

An emergency Board of Directors meeting was held by telephone that Thursday afternoon. It was resolved that Davidson would be fired and his office locked. On Friday morning when everyone returned from Los Angeles, a guard met Davidson at the door of his office and sent him to see me. I informed Davidson of the Board's resolution. Davidson was asked to turn in his company car keys and leave the building at once. It was September 24, 1982.

That same afternoon Porter Hurt came to Osborne Computer Corporation and met with Jim Ottinger, Jerry Petruzzelli, and myself. Hurt admitted that he did indeed have a relationship with the Access Matrix Microcomputer Company, but he assured everyone present that the Access Matrix computer was in a totally different price range and thus would never compete with any Osborne product. None of us believed Hurt, but we pretended otherwise and redoubled our efforts to find a second source for electronics boards.

Davidson and Osborne Computer Corporation subsequently sued each other. The thought that anyone would behave as Davidson had done never entered my mind and no agreement penalized anyone for such behavior. So Davidson got to keep his stock and parted with a mutually agreed upon out-of-court settlement.

At about the same time that Davidson left, the highly laudatory *60 Minutes* television program segment entitled "The Valley Boys" was screened in late September. The program devoted half of its hour to Osborne Computer Corporation, concentrating on the cast of unlikely characters responsible for this raging success. The program had been filmed six months earlier when the image portrayed was fair and accurate. At that time Jim Ottinger was the only member of the company's management team whose image fit the popular stereotype for his role.

The country was ready for the message delivered that September day. In the depths of a grinding recession, here was a story of astounding success surrounding very ordinary-looking people. One has to suppose that the *60 Minutes* crew are a canny lot, a group of seasoned professionals who keep their ratings high by sensing the public mood and accurately broadcasting what the public wants to see.

But the program received mixed reviews within the company. Georgette Psaris in particular was angry. She had spent two hours talking about women in business and ten seconds acknowledging that she expected to be rich. The ten seconds were broadcast.

Just about the time the *60 Minutes* program was being broadcast, the company ran into its next crisis.

The double density board that was supposed to be ready in April was finally finished in September. And it worked. Double density Osborne I's were shipped at the beginning of October, priced at $1995—but by the end of September ten thousand single density Osborne I's were still sitting unsold on dealers' shelves. Unless these units could be moved, and quickly, the company was in serious danger of having its distribution channels choked with unsellable goods. Dealers were estimating that more than eighty percent of the computers sold would be the double density machines, once the option was available.

Again Psaris' group met the challenge, working with Fred Brown and Lynn Hagen. Brown came up with the idea of adding dBASEII to the array of free programs given away with every Osborne I. This program would only be given away with single density machines until the backlog could be eliminated. Within two weeks a deal had been negotiated. Fred Brown's idea would cost Osborne Computer Corporation fifteen dollars per computer—or so the company thought—a small sum to pay per copy for this highly regarded program.

dBASEII is a "database manager," a program that stores on disk information of any kind, text or numbers. It then lets you find information, print reports, or look at comparative data on the screen. Using a data base you can keep mailing lists, customer lists, financial information, or whatever you want. Ashton-Tate, the company that owns dBASEII, had done an excellent job of promoting its product. It sold well, even though it is not easy to use.

Looking back, it is hard to say what effect, if any, the dBASEII free offer had on Osborne I sales in the fall of 1982, since this was the first year during which Osborne Computer Corporation could measure the impact of the Christmas selling season. In 1981 the company had been production bound. Dealers were all on allocation.

Table 8 shows actual recorded unit sales compared with the original 1981 business plan, the 1982 budget, and the modified 1982 budget following problems encountered earlier in the year.

Clearly there was a spectacular turnaround in sales, reflected in financial results for the quarters ending August and November of 1982, as shown in Tables 9 and 10.

Did Christmas cause the favorable results? Did the *60 Minutes* program help? Publicity from television must have contributed in some way to the company's sales success in the following months. Yet a survey

Table 8 **Comparison of projected and actual Osborne I sales for the second half of 1982.**

	1981 Plan	*1982 Budget*	*Revised 1982 Budget*	*Actual Sales*
July	4606	12450	6500	6502
August	4974	15250	8350	8413
September		18950	8750	9890
October		22800	10000	9403
November		26400	10700	9721
December		29500		12633

Table 9 **Income statement quarter end August 28, 1982.**

	Quarter End August 28, 1982 (In thousands except per-share amounts)
Net sales	$21,052
Cost of sales	15,289
Gross profit	5,763
Selling, general and administrative expenses	4,727
Research and development	462
Interest expense	284
Income (loss) before income taxes	290
Provision for income taxes	—
Net income (loss)	$290
Earnings (loss) per common and equivalent share	.12

Table 10 **Income statement quarter end November 27,1982.**

	Quarter end November 27, 1982 (in thousands, except per-share amounts)
Net sales	$29,014
Cost of sales	20,422
Gross profit	8,592
Selling, general, and administrative expenses	7,095
Research and development	851
Interest expense	348
Income (loss) before income taxes	298
Provision for income taxes	—
Net income (loss)	$298
Earnings (loss) per common and common equivalent share	.13

conducted by an independent research group in 1983 reflected some ambiguous and rather peculiar feedback.

According to this survey, the *60 Minutes* program had almost no discernible impact on sales. Less than one percent of Osborne computer buyers between October 1982 and January 1983 attributed their decision to media coverage of the company. And only seven percent of the respondents specifically identified the dBASEII software package as their reason for buying an Osborne I. Twenty-five percent of the sample cited free software that included dBASEII as their criterion to choose an Osborne computer. In fact, a large number of respondents claimed that free software in general (without any specific mention of dBASEII) induced them to select the Osborne I.

The survey institute concluded that the dBASEII offer was a huge success. On the other hand, so few consumers specifically cited dBASEII over software in general, it could also be argued that the dBASEII offer was a costly mistake that generated more headaches than sales.

And the headaches were certainly present. Bob Moody was in charge of the Osborne software group at the time. The dBASEII offer was scheduled to go into effect on October 4, 1982. But a few days earlier Moody decided that for "a couple of weeks" Osborne I buyers should receive a certificate entitling them to a free dBASEII rather than receiving the program itself. These two weeks would supposedly allow Ashton-Tate to provide Osborne with a tutorial program to help Osborne I owners learn dBASEII.

Unfortunately, Moody believed Ashton-Tate's claim that the tutorial programs were almost ready. Yet both Psaris and I knew the tried-and-true formula that any programmer's estimated completion time should be automatically doubled and moved up one scale in time. If Bob Moody had speculated that two weeks would become four months, he would have been closer to the truth: it was mid-January before any dBASEII packages were shipped. By then the chorus of disgruntlement and law-suit threats had hurt the company more than any free offer could have possibly helped.

To make matters worse, hundreds of people who had bought Osborne computers earlier wanted us to make the free dBASEII offer retroactive to some date just preceding their own purchases. Individuals who had bought their computers too long ago to make such a request without laughing at the same time reasoned that they should be given the free software package as a reward for being early buyers.

The market survey also gave the company its first solid evidence that owners did not like the five-inch screen. Fully fifty-three percent of the surveyed owners objected to it.

The end-of-November annual statement, prepared by Jim Ottinger and audited by Arthur Young, is shown later on in Table 14. It certainly looked like an annual statement that would generate an excellent public offering.

Despite the roar of positive publicity and impressive sales, the year ended on a somewhat less positive note than 1981. Having struggled for much of the year to find a president and other new senior managers, I was keenly aware of the difficulties that accompanied hypergrowth. Many truly talented individuals had been hired into supervisory or managerial spots for which they were well qualified. Yet in the three to six months required for employees to learn their jobs at Osborne, the jobs had outgrown them.

By November some people were getting tired. Psaris decided that she needed a vacation and requested a leave of absence. Employees were routinely working sixteen-hour days. It seemed like a treadmill that would never end. Only the expectation of a public offering and the prospect of immediate wealth kept them all going.

By now $10-million months became the expected target. The employee head count soared to eight hundred. The strain at every level of management became more intense with each passing week. In my Christmas address, I tempered the enthusiasm everyone felt for the company's success by warning that growth brought problems:

"People will not be allowed to remain in positions that have outgrown them," I warned, "and the policy begins with me."

A QUESTION OF NEW PRODUCTS

Nearly every microcomputer manufacturer has run into trouble introducing new products. Even Apple Computer Corporation has had more than its fair share of problems in this area. It reached the point where I would entertain public audiences by baiting Steve Jobs with the statement: "Apple is a company that was made by a computer, rather than ever having made a computer."

Apple abortively introduced the Apple III in 1978, then reintroduced it more than a year later, again with little commercial success. The company's Lisa computer has not done well either, and unless the Macintosh succeeds, Apple Computer Corporation's spectacular success will have resided entirely in the original Apple II and the updated versions of this venerable and aged product.

New product introductions become a problem to start-up companies because management is never willing to accept a simple truth: there are no short cuts. Small companies are under unbearable economic pressure—as was Osborne Computer Corporation—to make premature product introductions. Prior to a public offering, the typical one-product, high-growth, high-tech company cannot last a month without sales. And any number of uncontrollable contingencies can cause manufacturing or sales to stop. As this truth becomes more stark in the eyes of management, ever-greater pressure is applied to new product teams who resort to short cuts that are inevitably nothing more than premature introductions.

But given the size of my bank account, there was nothing I could have done, even if I had recognized the prematurity of the Osborne I when first introduced—which I did not. On the other hand, I did understand the difficulties haunting every hardware manufacturer's new product development program. A product that is introduced prematurely is an incomplete product. And when everyone is busy completing the incomplete, they have no time for anything new. I attempted to head this problem off by using outside consultants who were isolated from day-to-day production line engineering demands. As early as May of 1981 I started seeking qualified people. I talked to Mark Garretz (co author of a book with Sol Liebes for Osborne/McGraw-Hill) but Mark's payment demands were unreasonable. Then in September I found Fred Coury.

Coury is one of the better known Silicon Valley engineering consultants. He is a dark-haired, compelling individual of Lebanese heritage who speaks and acts with an intensity that demands attention. I developed a quick respect for this man and paid particular attention when he identified my engineering department as consisting of only a very few good people (Curt Ingraham for one) drowning in a sea of disorganization. Coury's criticisms were of immense concern to me since I already had prepared an ambitious new products and services program. It is summarized in the following undated strategy memo, which was distributed to the company's executive staff:

Development of New Markets:

Currently all company product is sold through computer stores. How fast should we develop alternate markets? Which market, if any, is likely to dominate in the future? As explained earlier, we intend to establish independent sales organizations, OEM customers, and national accounts. We also intend to penetrate the office equipment distribution market once this matures to the point where it can handle office computers effectively.

Within these categories, we must further establish policies for specific vertical markets. For example, with no assistance from us whatsoever, the Irish Republic Government chose our computer for their school system. Obviously a less expensive product that can be easily locked away is attractive to schools. Should we establish a special education task force? How about journalists? Lawyers? Should we leave such markets to independent sales organizations, should we handle them ourselves, or is the right distribution somewhere in between?

It is imperative that the vice-president of marketing address these questions early in 1982. It is imperative that we penetrate these various specialized markets without undermining our dealer base.

Development of New Products:

When developing new products we will bear in mind these two overriding strategy considerations:
1. We must fight inevitable competition by rendering it obsolete as soon as it is announced. This means we must have products waiting to be announced with better price/performance.
2. New products must not impact existing products by drying up sales in anticipation of the new announcement or by leaving us with a large useless inventory.

We will offer an injection-molded case beginning in May. This case will become the standard housing for the OSBORNE 1, 2 & 3. People who own OSBORNE 1's with vacuum-formed cases will be able to upgrade to an injection molded case for a fee.

The OSBORNE 2 will look identical to the OSBORNE 1; however, it will have enhanced electronics. OSBORNE 1 owners will be able to upgrade to the OSBORNE 2. People who bought the OSBORNE 1 in advance of the OSBORNE 2 will be able to upgrade for almost the same price as having bought an OSBORNE 2 in the first place. People who buy an OSBORNE 1 after the OSBORNE 2 is announced will be able to upgrade for a small overall surcharge.

The OSBORNE 3 will use essentially the same electronics as the OSBORNE 2; however, it will offer a larger screen and it will use slimline diskette drives.

Marketing strategy for the OSBORNE 1, 2 & 3 has been discussed in executive session.

The OSBORNE 4 will be introduced early in 1983 as a shocking new low-priced product. This, too, has been discussed in executive session.

Approved Software List:

Considerable revenues can be derived selling additional software to existing OSBORNE 1 owners. In the future, we anticipate software accounting for a much larger percentage of overall revenues than shown in 1982 income and profit summaries. It is important that we consolidate our position as the principal supplier of OSBORNE 1 additional software before the magnitude becomes apparent to outside vendors. This will be done using the Approved Software List.

Generally, a program will go on the Approved Software List if we have exclusive rights to market the program to OSBORNE 1 customers. We will attempt to cover a broad range of applications, but have very few directly competing software packages on this Approved List.

The Magazine:

We will publish an end user magazine beginning in 1982. Given the size of the potential customer base, the magazine could have a significant circulation by late 1982. The principal reason for having a magazine is to establish excellent contact with OSBORNE 1 owners. However, it should certainly pay for itself and could generate an interesting profit. The magazine will be aimed at Z80/CP/M computers broadly to increase its circulation and to attract good articles. I will resurrect my ''From the Fountainhead'' column for the magazine. The magazine will carry advertising.

Customer Service:

Our aim is to sell computers in high volume to consumers. Therefore, it is imperative that we have excellent customer service available. It is our policy to insist that dealers support their own customers; however, wherever our choice is to let a customer suffer from a delinquent dealer or support the customer with our own personnel, the choice is clear. We must support the customer ourselves, and we must have the staff to handle the task.

Hardware Service:

Unlike customer service, hardware service is a revenue center. Service contracts will be sold to owners of computers that are out of warranty. We anticipate the service profit center accounting for an interesting percentage of profits during 1981. In future years, service is likely to generate a smaller percentage of total profits, since software is likely to become an increasing profit contributor. For the same reason that a strong customer service department is needed, we must maintain excellent hardware service personnel, and we must build a reputation for reliability and support.

But more urgent than new products, some obvious Osborne I improvements had to be addressed immediately:

1. Get an injection-molded plastic case. The cheap-looking vacuum-formed case used by the Osborne I when introduced won users' hearts only as an ugly duckling, or more precisely, perhaps, as an ugly World War II army combat radio. It was, in fact, twice as expensive as its more professional-looking injection-molded counterpart.
2. Provide a double-density upgrade for the disk drives.
3. Display eighty characters per line in contrast to the existing fifty-two-character lines. Although an eighty-column display on a five-inch screen would be readable only to literate ants with perfect vision, eighty percent of Osborne I customers were using a larger external monitor that could display eighty characters legibly.

Initially Osborne Computer Corporation had planned to start shipping double-density upgrades by December of 1981 and eighty-column upgrades shortly thereafter. It was October of 1982 before the double-density option was available, while the eighty-column upgrade was not introduced until January of 1983. These were the company's first major delays, and they hurt our credibility because the press had already quoted my more optimistic delivery dates.

The eighty-column option would have been introduced even later than January of 1983, if at all, but for a small Australian company that showed up at Osborne Computer Corporation in September of 1982 with their own working eighty-column upgrade board. In fact their board doubled the number of characters per line from fifty-two to one hundred and four. Users had the option of eliminating ten characters on the left and right sides of the screen to reduce the display to eighty characters. This display was totally unreadable on the five-inch monitor but very clear on a larger external monitor. Moreover, people using spreadsheets found the screen with one hundred and four characters very attractive since it would allow more of the spreadsheet to be displayed.

The engineering department rejected the Australian eighty-column upgrade board, saying that it would not work. The Aussies then confronted me personally. Still smarting from the double density upgrade fiasco, I was totally disillusioned with Ed Richter and ordered that the board be used. This decision did not go over well with the engineers who would now have to make the board run.

The real new products program began in the fall of 1981 with products then described as the Osborne II, III, and IV.

The Osborne III was given the code name "Shelly." It was eventually introduced in April of 1983 as the "Executive," and was to be an enhanced Osborne I with more capabilities and a larger screen, but the same general appearance. It was the product for Osborne I owners who wanted to trade up, or for buyers who found that the Osborne I did not do enough for them.

The Osborne II was going to be an Osborne I with Shelly electronics. This product was code named "Tresca," but the Shelly logic board and software was so late (it ultimately became the critical path item delaying the Executive introduction) that this option was never offered.

The Osborne IV was built under the code name "Vixen." It was never introduced. Vixen was to be electronically compatible with the Osborne I, but as small and inexpensive as possible.

Both the Shelly and the Vixen were to use "slim line" disk drives. These were half the thickness and a little more than half the price of the standard drives in the Osborne I (and in the IBM PC.)

Wherever possible common components were to be used in all Osborne products.

The Vixen was to have a five-inch screen, since this product was to be as small as possible. The Executive was given a seven-inch screen since it was looked on as a transition product. "Portable" computers with a nine-inch screen are all too large and heavy to be really portable—"transportable" is more accurate. I believed (and still believe) that the seven-inch screen is the ideal size for a portable computer. The Shelly kept the Osborne I outer case only to save time and tooling costs. As soon as possible it would be redesigned to be more attractive and to make the best possible use of a seven-inch screen.

Ultimately, it was the Shelly electronics that became the critical path item, determining the product's introduction date. Moreover, the Vixen case, originally designed for a five-inch monitor, was found to be capable of housing a seven-inch monitor.

Although IBM had already introduced its personal computer, the Shelly and Vixen were designed to be CP/M machines, compatible with the Osborne I. At the time I did not believe that IBM would be as quickly and overwhelmingly successful as they were.

Building an industry-standard computer running industry-standard software was not IBM's style. IBM had already tried to enter the personal computer market ahead of everyone else with their highly unsuccessful model 5100. Also, IBM had never sold a really successful minicomputer. So if you think IBM would be successful selling a cardboard box with their initials on it, you're wrong—as the PCjr may yet prove.

IBM succeeded in the personal computer market because they were smart. Their program managers should be commended for their good judgement. Just being IBM is no guarantee of success. They broke away from their past by buying industry-standard microprocessor chips from Intel, rather than designing their own. They also talked to Digital Research about the CP/M operating system and to Microsoft about their MS-DOS operating system instead of writing their own proprietary software. But would they also sell through computer stores, positioning their product as a minicomputer? Yes. IBM played their hand brilliantly.

Because of Osborne Computer Corporation's many crises, new product development moved slowly until the hypergrowth second half of 1982. Then at last there was a significant improvement in the new product introduction schedules.

One midsummer day Jim Ottinger found me sitting in my office in total despair. I had just ended one more meeting with the new products project management team, who once again could report only that every schedule had slipped one week since the previous week's meeting.

Ottinger suggested that Al Stone be moved out of the international department and be put in charge of new products. Stone's methods may have lacked finesse but he got things done. The move would end the constant bickering between Stone and Mike McCullough. So in the summer of 1982, Stone moved out of the international department and took over project management of the Shelly and the Vixen.

In July of 1982 the plan was that the Shelly would replace the Osborne I at the double density unit's $1995 retail price, while the Vixen would be introduced at $1495. By September the marketing department was proposing that the Shelly be introduced at $2495 and the Vixen at $1695.

In November of 1982, we hoped that Shelly boards would be available, so Osborne I owners could upgrade to Shelly capabilities. This, recall, was the Tresca product. Although the double density upgrade had finally been taken care of, the company had by then essentially given up on an eighty-column upgrade for the Osborne I. Shelly boards would have to substitute.

"Wayne" was another new product whose development began in the fall of 1982. Wayne was to be the office typewriter replacement, taking up no more space than a typewriter.

Wayne was designed to have a nine-inch screen, two slim line disk drives, and a printer sitting on the back of the unit where a typewriter's printing mechanism is usually located. Wayne would use Vixen circuitry, since it was to provide low-cost word processing, electronic spreadsheets, and communications. The entire unit, including printer, was to retail for $1995.

But problems persisted. The Shelly (Executive) logic board seemed to have an endless series of problems.

During 1982 a month was lost when Osborne Computer Corporation abandoned the house that had laid out and manufactured most of our printed circuit boards in the past. To save money, a cheaper, untested organization was chosen. This new group went bankrupt halfway through the job. When they finally delivered the Shelly printed circuit board—very late—it was full of errors and almost worthless. So in November of 1982 it was decided that the Shelly/Executive and the Vixen would both be introduced at the end of February. Then it was agreed that the Vixen would have to be introduced two months later, in April, to avoid manufacturing and production line congestion.

By early January the Shelly introduction was being delayed again. Now the goal was to introduce the product at the 1983 West Coast Computer Faire, in mid-March. The schedule called for production boards to start flowing at the beginning of March, allowing a small inventory to be established by the middle of the month. But as the days rolled by and deadlines for magazine advertising and publicity articles approached, Psaris decided to add a month to the Executive introduction schedule. April 17 was selected.

Then in January of 1983 Al Stone showed everyone that a seven-inch display would fit in the Vixen case. But it was May of 1983 before the seven-inch Vixen was given the company's full blessing. Under John Hanne's expert control, this product became the first Osborne microcomputer designed with manufacturing in mind.

Estimates showed that the seven-inch Vixen could be assembled in eleven minutes. But by the summer of 1983 there was a strong body of opinion throughout the company that even a seven-inch Vixen introduced in the fall of 1983 would not be successful, since it was a CP/M-based machine. The world had gone to IBM so totally, this body of opinion reasoned, that the Vixen should be postponed yet again until it could be given IBM PC compatibility. This was a rather dubious analysis, given the sales levels being achieved by Kaypro, whose products would have been overwhelmed by the Vixen.

In the fall of 1982 it was obvious to all but the blind that the IBM PC had established a new industry standard. I decided to offer a version of the Executive that would be IBM PC compatible. I had no intention of developing an IBM compatible computer in-house, given the company's dismal record in engineering development. So I started hunting for an outside group to handle the task at a reasonable price. A small San Diego company called PCPI was located.

Interestingly enough, the first contact with this group was made in Holland at the European Comdex show in the fall of 1982. PCPI already had an IBM compatible logic board for the Apple II. By November of 1982 Osborne Computer Corporation got them to start work on an IBM compatible upgrade for the Shelly.

By May of 1983 it had also become clear that PCPI would be unable to deliver product. The prototypes they made were expensive, late, and included wholly unacceptable features, such as circles that would be displayed as ovals when an Executive user switched from CP/M to IBM compatibility.

John Hanne, who had been hired as vice president of engineering in April of 1983, and Ron Ogg, who was in charge of software products, looked for a substitute. The substitute was a board designed by MAD Computers, plus system software from another company who demanded anonymity.

Osborne's programming and engineering staff did considerable work both on the MAD board and on the purchased software. At the beginning of September, 1983, precisely at the time the company was filing for bankruptcy, the first prototypes of the IBM compatible Executives were being built.

It looked as though the machine was as close to being one hundred percent IBM compatible as one could get without stealing the proprietary IBM "read-only memory" (ROM) chips.

The term "IBM compatible" means a lot of different things to a lot of different people. For example, Felsenstein and I had visited Sanyo, the Japanese electronics manufacturer, early in 1983 and were shown a microcomputer that used the 8088 microprocessor, which is also used by the IBM PC. That was the only similarity between the IBM and Sanyo products. Not a single IBM program would have run on the Sanyo microcomputer without first making program changes. My Japanese hosts wanted to know what I thought of their soon-to-be-introduced product.

"To sell in America, it must be IBM compatible," I replied.

So it was—which is not to say that Sanyo modified their microcomputer in any way; they just claimed IBM compatibility based on the shared microcomputer chip.

IBM compatibility is like pregnancy. You are or you are not. There are no shades of gray. To be IBM compatible, it must be possible to take a program disk out of an IBM microcomputer any program disk—and run the program on the compatible microcomputer without requiring any program modification.

In addition to sharing the same microprocessor, the compatible microcomputer must handle the screen and all external devices (such as printers and modems) exactly as the IBM PC does. The hardest part is writing that piece of the operating system software that resides in a chip on the computer logic board. This program must look externally exactly like the IBM equivalent, but to avoid copyright infringement the program itself must be totally different. It is at this point that most "compatible" microcomputers cease to be compatible.

But despite rumors to the contrary, there is life after IBM. During 1984 and 1985 a number of "lap computers" will be introduced—none of which can be truly IBM compatible, even though most will likely make this claim. Compatibility will be impossible because these lap computers will all have smaller screens and will use different disk storage devices.

In May and June of 1983, I worked with Felsenstein lining up a Japanese manufacturer to build a lap-sized computer to introduce in mid-1984. The computer was to have an eighty-character, sixteen-row flat screen (liquid crystal) display, one three-inch micro floppy disk drive, 64K bytes of memory, a cartridge for programs, an IBM compatible 8088 microprocessor, a modem, plus connectors for printers, more disk drives, and additional peripherals. The whole thing would run on batteries. It would be built in Japan, and would cost us under $600 each, delivered to Hayward, California. It would have sold for $1995. But don't weep if you want one; there will be a buffalo herd on such products on the market before 1984 is over.

I had always considered software a very important component of the company's business. Having started with bundled software, I planned to acquire exclusive rights for a variety of programs that would then be marketed to a captive audience.

The acquisitions program got off to a brisk, but ill-planned start under Thom Hogen, a man with an immense and accurate understanding of microcomputer software, who in my opinion is far better at starting projects than he is at finishing them. Beginning in late 1981, Thom identified some excellent programs for which he obtained exclusive Osborne I rights. Unfortunately, by mid-1982 enthusiasm and inexperience were running neck-and-neck within Hogen's software group. Deals were being made faster than the existing backlog of acquired titles could be taken to market. Also, two deals were concluded whereby Osborne Computer Corporation paid excessive advances to two companies: Softech and Peachtree.

Under terms of the first contract Softech provided Osborne with the UCSD Pascal, a very popular programming language, plus development software for people who wanted to write their own Pascal programs on the Osborne I. The second contract committed Osborne to buy a large amount of business software from Peachtree, for resale to Osborne I owners. On signing their contracts with Osborne Computer Corporation, these two companies must have celebrated long and hard.

Both agreements could have been quite profitable to Osborne, and in the absence of the bankruptcy probably would have been. The problem was that Thom Hogen's group agreed that Osborne would make all necessary modifications so that the programs in question would run on Osborne microcomputers—but they made no subsequent plans to implement these modifications. The company's software group was overcommitted already, so UCSD Pascal was not available for the Osborne I until September of 1983, and Peachtree business software was never sold to Osborne owners, despite endless customer demand for such programs.

Bob Moody finally replaced Thom Hogen, but this change of command did not alleviate the problem. When Ron Ogg took charge of the software department in April of 1983, things finally started to move.

My 1981 memo talked about a company magazine. *The Portable Companion* was the result. It became an excellent, well-designed and useful magazine packed with information. It got a quick following and soon acquired 25,000 paying subscribers. Even following the company's bankruptcy, subscription renewals continued briskly. Today it is in circulation again; neither its staff nor its customers would let it die.

A QUESTION OF PRICING—THE HYPERGROWTH MODEL

Hypergrowth occurs in markets that are unsaturated. On a pie chart of participants, the largest slice would have to be marked: "Waiting for something to buy." In a hypergrowth environment there are no real competitors; market share is there for the taking. One company does not increase its sales by taking market share from another.

Perhaps the best way to analyze hypergrowth is to look at a mathematical model of sales in such an environment, and then look at how the model changes as market saturation is approached.

Within a hypergrowth environment I have found that the following equation fairly measures sales volume as a function of retail price:

$$V = VS * 10\text{exp}\left[-2*((P-PS)/(PH-PS))\right]$$

where

V is the number of units sold per time period at a unit price of *P*.

VS is the target number of units to be sold in the same time period, at a target price of *PS*.

PH is the high price at which sales of the product are extinguished, which is to say that sales are reduced to 1% of *PS*.

This equation represents a straight line drawn on semilog graph paper with price as the linear coordinate.

The principal hypergrowth characteristic of this equation is the lack of any upper boundary on sales dampening what appears to be an inexorable upward climb in sales volume *(V)* as unit price *(P)* declines. Figure 1 shows how sales can climb relentlessly to astounding heights as the price of a product falls within a hypergrowth environment (represented by the smooth line). Once market saturation appears, the apparently infinite upside sales potential begins to be forced back to a finite boundary (represented by the broken line). Now as prices fall, sales asymptotically approach this boundary instead of reaching for infinity.

Figure 1 uses imaginary data, both for prices and for unit volumes; however, this data would probably fit some software packages currently being shipped.

In a hypergrowth environment a company strives for sales volume rather than market share.

The microcomputer industry operated in a hypergrowth environment until quite recently. Now that IBM has soaked up the bulk of that large pie slice labeled "waiting for something to buy," companies are battling for market share. As the upper boundary on potential sales acquires a definable value, the hypergrowth environment disappears and is replaced by the more typical competitive environment known to manufacturers of soap, canned peas, or automobiles. In this situation one

Figure 1 **Price Volume Relationship for Some Arbitrary Microcomputer Product.**

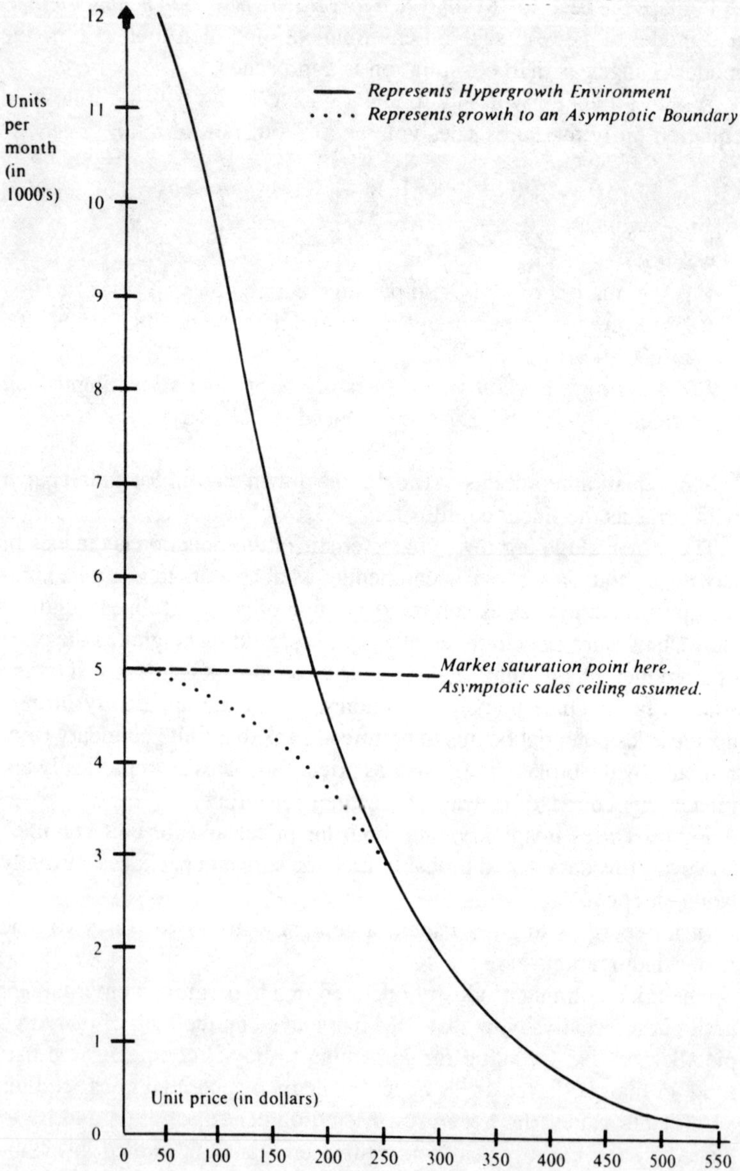

company increases its sales volume largely at the expense of another company.

The hypergrowth market may appear to be a manager's dream, but in truth its unique complexities make it a very difficult environment within which to operate successfully.

VS (target volume) and *PS* (target price) are the two most important parameters to any hypergrowth company, since these two numbers are not fixed. There is no "universal" relationship that defines one value for sales volume *(VS)* that any company participating in a hypergrowth market will achieve for any product priced at *PS*. On the contrary, *VS* and *PS* are very volatile: they move quickly in response to customer demand for product. But for given values of *VS* and *PS*, all other combinations of *V* and *P* are defined.

The goal of management in any hypergrowth company therefore is to maximize *VS*, which translates specifically into maximizing customer perception of the company's product as being "the product to buy." And this is what leads to the high instability of hypergrowth companies, because growth rate itself is the factor that most immediately influences customer perceptions. High growth rate brings customers storming into retail outlets. They all want to be part of "the action." A pause or a brief decline in a company's fortunes drives customers away in equivalent droves. This undesirable reality can be represented over short time periods by the following differential mathematical relationship:

$$VS = K1 \frac{\mathrm{d}\,VS}{\mathrm{d}\,PS} + \mathrm{f}(PS, VS)$$

where
K1 is a constant, and
f*(PS, VS)* is a slow-moving function for simplicity assumed to equal another constant, *K2*.

This generally translates into the rule that the faster you are growing, the faster you will grow.

But f*(PS, VS)* is not really a constant. It includes two integral terms. The first is the sum of "recent" sales representing a market segment whose product needs have been satisfied. This first integral term is negative, reducing the value of *VS*. The second integral term is the sum of "mature" sales, representing the customer base that is ready to reorder. This second integral term kicks in much later and tends to increase *VS*.

During a hypergrowth company's infancy, when it has no installed base, f*(PS,VS)* is a constant. Then the first integral function kicks in, damping down VS. By the time the second integral kicks in, the hypergrowth phase of the market is probably ending, and the equations degenerate to the more classical price-volume curves of companies competing for market share.

It is therefore critical for a new company to achieve a very high growth rate very early in its product cycle. This task becomes increasingly difficult as the product becomes more mature.

But the most important and frequently missed goal in any company, whether or not it operates in a hypergrowth environment, is to seek maximum gross profit. It is easy to do a land sale business selling dollar bills for ninety-nine cents each. Racking up huge unit sales and net revenues within a hypergrowth environment does no company a bit of good if every sale translates into a net dollar loss. That is self-evident. What is not so self-evident is the fact that simply making a profit on each sale is not good enough either. Sales strategy must aim at making the maximum gross profit. In other words, sales strategy must maximize the product of total unit sales multiplied by gross profit per sale.

Here we define "gross profit" as "net revenue less cost of goods." "Cost of goods" is the amount it cost to manufacture, warehouse, and ship the product. "Net revenues" is the total amount of revenue received from the sale of goods, less reserves taken for returns or special discounts that may subsequently reduce the net revenue.

"Cost of goods" can usually be represented by a formula that includes two components: a fixed cost and a variable cost. This may be illustrated as follows:

$$CG = FC/V + VC$$

where
CG represents cost of goods in dollars per unit
FC represents total fixed-cost dollars per month
V represents unit sales per month
VC represents variable costs in dollars per unit

The fixed cost takes into account direct overhead on labor. The variable component itself can be broken down into two parts: direct labor, which does not vary much with volume, and part costs (also called "bill of materials"), which does.

$$VC = DL + PC$$

where
DL represents direct labor in dollars per unit
PC represents part costs, also as dollars per unit

Manufacturers of automobiles or canned peas never see sales volumes change very dramatically; therefore they can use fairly simple formulas to represent the change in part costs as a function of sales volume. But when sales volumes vary as widely as the hypergrowth environment allows, something more sophisticated is required. I have found this variation of the price-volume equation works well:

$$PC = (\log V - K3)/K4$$

where $K3$ and $K4$ are empirical constants.

By calculating cost of goods as a function of sales volume, it is now possible to show how a company can be better off increasing their prices and selling lower unit volumes because volume and profit change at different rates. If the rate at which sales volume increases is insufficient to offset the loss in profit that accompanies a lower unit price, then there is no point in looking for higher volume.

If gross profit is plotted against unit price, usually the peak of the gross profit curve is very flat, as shown in Table 11, which compares gross profit with price for the Osborne I and the Osborne Executive.

The constants for the Executive in this table assume a steady state (non-start-up) condition where more than one product is being manufactured. In this case the Executive bears a large part, but not all, of the fixed overhead cost (*FC*). The Executive sales volume data are high when compared to sales recorded in the summer of 1983, in the absence of any discernible sales or marketing program, but the numbers are probably realistic for twelve selling months averaged out, with proper marketing and advertising support.

It pays to pick a price on the rising (high-priced) slope of the gross profit curve since lower sales volume means fewer headaches. Also, it means the first effect of a price war will be to raise your gross profit.

Consequently, the correct double density Osborne I price in 1982 probably was $1995, while the correct introductory price for the Executive was probably $2195. Table 11 shows a larger percentage gross profit for the Osborne I than actually recorded in 1982 and as reported in Tables 9 and 10. This is because various inefficiencies and inventory write offs are included in the numbers actually achieved. But management's task is to remove inefficiencies and manage inventory to eliminate excessive write offs—a goal that can only be asymptotically approached in a hypergrowth environment. Pricing should be based on an efficient operation.

Table 11 **Analysis of sales price and gross profit for Osborne I and Executive.**

Double Density Osborne I Data (1982)

Estimated values:	Average discount:		63%	*FC:*	400000
VS:	9000	*DL:*	35		
PS:	$1995	*PC:*	$641	at *VS*	unit volume
PH:	$4995	*PC:*	$850	at *VS*/100	unit volume

Price $:	1197	1596	1995	2145	2295
Units/month:	30637	16605	9000	7149	5679
Net revenues:	23103470	16696135	11311650	9660739	8210427
Unit COG $:	633.46	672.29	720.44	742.40	767.34
Total COG $:	19407216	11163501	6484000	5307400	4357428
Gross profit:	3696254	5532634	4827650	4353340	3853000

Executive (1983)

Estimated values:					
Average discount:	63	*FC:*	275000		
VS:	9000	*DL:*	15		
PS:	1995	*PC:*	797	at *VS*	unit volume
PH:	4995	*PC:*	1050	at *VS*/100	unit volume

Price $:	1596	1995	2145	2295	2445
Units/ month:	16605	9000	7149	5679	4511

Net revenues:	16696135	11311650	9660739	8210427	6948034
Unit COG $:	794.91	842.56	863.12	885.73	910.92
Total COG $:	13199626	7583000	6170385	5029705	4108857
Gross profit:	3496509	3728650	3490354	3180722	2839177

The Executive would never have been as profitable in 1983 as the Osborne I had been in 1982. However, Osborne Computer Corporation was paying far too much for Executive cost of goods, as shown in Table 12. Nevertheless, given the existing price structure, the company would have needed its other two products, the Vixen and the IBM PC compatible Executive, to maintain its profitability.

According to my price-volume formula, a target sales volume *(VS)* for a specified retail price *(PS)* is chosen and then the extinguishing price *(PH)*—that is, the higher price at which sales will drop to just one percent of the previously assumed volume—is estimated.

The value of this approach is that it focuses sharply on the critical issue: achieving the maximum sales volume at any particular target price. Assuming that a desired sales volume can be achieved for the target price, it is then possible to determine whether the price should in fact be increased or decreased to achieve maximum gross profit.

Osborne I and Executive pricing were sources of great friction at Osborne Computer Corporation in the months prior to bankruptcy. In the absence of any advertising campaign, and surrounded by gloomy press, Executive sales dropped to 2500 units per month by July of 1983. Sales then increased dramatically when the price was lowered in test markets to $1995—more than three times as many computers were sold. The gross profit analysis for the Executive during the summer of 1983 according to my formula follows:

Price $:	1497	1996	2495	2620	2745
Units/month:	15716	6268	2500	1986	1577
Net revenues:	14821848	7882085	3929625	3277795	2727865
Unit COG $:	728.50	805.37	922.00	963.13	1011.64
Total COG $:	11449062	5048211	2305000	1912607	1595751
Gross profit:	3372786	2833874	1624625	1365189	1132114

These numbers starkly demonstrate the need for bold pricing action in a crisis.

Osborne I sales, meanwhile, were sinking to desperately low levels. I wanted the Osborne I price to be reduced to $1495 when the Executive was introduced. By early May it was clear that a retail price of even $1495 was too high. The street price for the double density Osborne I had already fallen to $1295. From mid-May on, Joe Roebuck, Jim Ottinger, and I campaigned for the Osborne I price to be reduced to $1295. Here is the appropriate Osborne I gross profit data for the summer of 1983:

Price $:	897	1196	1495	1545
Units/month:	15704	3963	1000	794
Net revenues:	8874277	2985876	941850	773159
Unit COG $:	556.94	666.60	916.00	991.18
Total COG $:	8745945	2641574	916000	787323
Gross profit:	128332	344302	25850	14164

Ignoring reserve accounts, there was not much profit left in the Osborne I by the summer of 1983, but the correct retail price probably was $1295. The Osborne I price was finally reduced to $1295 in August, but the Executive price remained at $2495 until the company's bankruptcy.

Jaunich argued that the Executive price could not be reduced from $2495 because it was simply too expensive to manufacture. But Jaunich was basing his argument on the cost of goods computed for the first month of the Executive's manufacture, which was no basis for long-term pricing.

Clearly cost of goods could be reduced dramatically in the months to come. And there was indeed plenty of room for cost reduction. Osborne Computer Corporation without Tom Davidson was overpaying for the components that went into the Executive and should have renegotiated contracts with major suppliers. Table 12 shows the cost of goods for the Executive and indicates its dependency on both the volume of production and on the component costs.

In May of 1983 Executive cost of sales initially totaled more than $1000 because of start-up expenses. (The numbers shown in Table 12 are best estimates after elimination of start-up costs.) Also, the company had received an offer from Samsung, the Korean electronics manufacturer, to build Executives in Korea. The landed price in Hayward, plus local added costs, would have produced a total cost of sales of roughly $730.

Furthermore, it came to light during these Executive pricing arguments that Osborne Computer Corporation's labor overhead was artificially inflated. Rent and utilities were being allocated throughout the company on the basis of occupied floor space rather than on improvements or on actual utilization of overhead services. Errors of this type are more important than management realizes, since overhead entering cost of goods gets multiplied by three or four when determining retail price; whereas overhead appearing below the gross profit line does not.

Table 12 **Executive cost of sales (initial and after first reductions).**

Cost of Sales	*June*	*September*
Bill of Materials:		
Main logic board	$238	
128K memory board	110	
Main logic board with on-board memory		343
Disk drives with electronics	232	
Disk drives		130
Custom disk electronics		30
7-inch display with power supply	70	70
Keyboard with cables	39	39
Plastic case	45	45
Other	36	36
Total bill of materials	770	693
Direct labor and overhead	77	61
Software royalties	11	5
Other cost of sales	40	38
Total cost of sales	898	797
Net revenue based on $2495 price	1550	1550
Gross margin	652	753
%	42	48.6
Net Revenue Based on $1995 price	1237	1237
Gross margin	338	440
%	27.3	35.6

Part II THE FALL

Chapter Six NEW MANAGEMENT

Michael Schulhof was my choice for a new company president.

He had recently stepped down from the position of president of Sony Corporation of America, and was interested; but after visiting the New Jersey Osborne facility, he warned prophetically that Osborne Computer Corporation should not hire him or anyone else to be president. Schulhof recognized that the company was still running on a high energy level that a new president would destroy, causing the company problems. He therefore declined the position.

It was Bob Jaunich who would become president of the Corporation.

I was introduced to Jaunich by Jim Ottinger in August of 1982.

"This hunt for a new president is going very slowly," I griped to Jim one day.

"You know, you might just try calling Bob Jaunich," Jim suggested. "He's an executive vice president at Consolidated Foods, but from what I hear he may be interested in a move." Jim then explained that he had worked for Jaunich at Memorex.

"If he is an executive vice president, running half of a multibillion-dollar corporation, why would he leave it for a high-risk, high-tech start-up company like Osborne?" I asked.

"Because he still lives here in Silicon Valley but works in Chicago," Ottinger replied.

"So all he has to do is move to Chicago," I noted.

"Would you move to Chicago?" Ottinger asked with a chuckle. A chauvinistic and unconvincing response, but it was definitely worth a telephone call.

The preliminary telephone conversation was very encouraging, so I met Jaunich a couple of times in the fall of 1982 at my Hayward offices and at the Dunfey Hotel in San Mateo. I was impressed . . . very impressed. His demeanor convinced me that he was brilliant. Dvorak notes that Jaunich elicits the same description from everyone he meets: "He's really intelligent," they invariably say. Ask how they know and they typically respond: "You can just tell." Jaunich impresses people.

By then it was already October and I was growing desperate. I had postponed hiring additional vice presidents except in absolutely critical areas so that the new president could participate in the selection process. But every week that a new president was not hired, the strains on existing management grew more severe. Hiring a new president had become my top priority.

Jaunich telephoned me a few days after the meeting at the Dunfey. "I think it's worth exploring further," he said.

I was delighted and somewhat surprised. Jaunich's major concern, according to Jim Ottinger, was that I really did not intend to relinquish control of my company. Jaunich had no interest in accepting a position where his authority would constantly be undermined by the Board chairman. In fact, Jaunich had turned down offers from both Apple and Atari. Both had offered him top management positions, but in neither case did he have confidence that he would be allowed to do things his way.

I, however, was ready to relinquish management of my company to a seasoned professional such as Jaunich. Growth had taken Osborne Computer Corporation to a size where I had to question my own qualifications. I had no professional training whatsoever in finance, management, or business administration, the very disciplines within which I was making critical decisions every day. Psaris had already told me that she was close to burning out. As entrepreneurs Psaris and I had done our part.

Moreover, neither power nor vast sums of money motivate me. I do what I do because it is a challenge—and it is fun. Never have I felt there was any big thrill associated with heading a large company. It is just endless work—very hard work. At about the time Ottinger described Jaunich's concerns, I met a personal friend from my pre-Osborne Computer days. I remember him sitting wide-eyed in my office, after a tour of the facility.

"Christ!" he said. "What does it feel like to head of all this?"

I don't remember my response, but I do remember not understanding the question, and then slowly realizing the significance of my incomprehension.

So when in November of 1982 I requested the Board of Directors to consider Jaunich's candidacy, I did so ready and willing to let him take my place.

Serious negotiations immediately got under way between Jaunich and Osborne Computer Corporation's Board. Jack Melchor and Ken Oshman negotiated on behalf of the company. The two major issues were stock and authority. In particular Jaunich wanted a timetable for his appointment as chief executive officer; he would only stay on three to six months in the position of chief operating officer, and that was all.

I was intoxicated with the wonder of someone as powerful as Jaunich taking the reins of my company. "Surely he will grow it into a billion-dollar company," I repeated to all who listened. And (naively) I even attempted to establish some type of understanding with Jaunich, as one human being to another. At his club one Saturday, I talked about trust and understanding—only to be met with a slightly puzzled smile, lightly overlaid with amusement. But I would not be discouraged.

In early December negotiations were complicated when Consolidated Foods promoted Jaunich to the position of chief operating officer. I received the news with a sinking heart. Surely our negotiations would now come to a fast end. I called Jaunich to offer congratulations and was amazed to discover that he was still interested in the Osborne position, but not as chief operating officer.

Why, he mused, should he move from chief operating officer of Consolidated Foods to a similar position at a tiny company like Osborne? Jaunich wanted to be chief executive officer. So negotiations continued through Christmas, with Jack Melchor and Ken Oshman talking to Jaunich. Meanwhile, I married Barbara Burdick, and we left on our honeymoon as negotiations continued.

In the first days of January, just when it looked as though we finally had a deal, Jaunich came forward with the news that Consolidated Foods had offered him an immediate $1-million-dollar cash bonus to stay. Like a good salesman, Jaunich was putting the pressure on us—and raising the stakes.

I met with Jack Melchor, Ken Oshman, and Les Hogan in Ken's Rolm Corporation office. The deciding issue had become control; a solution had to be found. Ken finally suggested that the problem could be solved if Jaunich was hired into the company immediately as chief executive officer.

I knew Jaunich would replace me, but I wanted to stay in charge of the company as chief executive until the new machines—the Executive and the Vixen—had been introduced, and a public stock offering had occurred. I felt that a smooth new product introduction was critical to the company.

New product transitions have been pregnant with danger for all microcomputer manufacturers who have one or perhaps two products that account for nearly all their income. Switching to a new principal source of income is like climbing a rock face, throwing away your boots halfway up and counting on a new, improved pair for the rest of the climb. You're putting a lot of confidence in the new boots.

Osborne Computer Corporation had smoothly handled the transition from vacuum-formed brown case to injection-molded blue case units, and then from single density to double density computers. But those were small transitions—exchanging shoe laces—compared with dropping the Osborne I entirely and replacing it with two new machines. We were now talking about new boots!

I insisted it was extremely dangerous to have new and inexperienced management make critical decisions in the throes of such a product transition. "Let Jaunich watch and then take over in May," I argued.

This issue brought negotiations to a standstill. Jaunich demanded a fast schedule for his promotion to chief executive officer, with guarantees surrounding this transition. The guarantees halted negotiations.

"Bob Jaunich is not so foolish as to ignore the existing management," Ken reassured. "And if there is a conflict, the Board will be behind you," he added. Everyone agreed.

Faced with the awesome prospect of starting all over in my hunt for a president, I deferred.

During the second week of January 1983, Jaunich started work at Osborne Computer Corporation as president and chief executive officer at $150,000 a year—$20,000 less than my salary as chairman of the board. He would also receive options to purchase 100,000 shares of stock at the prevailing estimated price of $16 per share. On a public offering, he would be allowed to register 30,000 shares and to sell 20,000 of them, thereby covering his option price and providing an offset for the $1-million bonus that Consolidated Foods had offered him as a last-ditch effort to prevent his departure.

For the balance of January it looked as though the transition would indeed be smooth. Jaunich changed nothing. He attended meetings, asked questions, and rarely intervened. The only complaint he voiced to me was that the Board had been a little parsimonious on the subject of his stock options.

Beginning in February Jaunich quickly took charge. He made it clear that most of the old management would go, along with old methods of operation and old management style.

Jaunich and I are as different as two men can be. This became abundantly clear within weeks of his arrival and was subsequently reinforced in the few conversations we ever had as one human being to another.

Jaunich is closed, analytical, and intense. I am open, intuitive, and generally easygoing. Jaunich has a vicious temper that constantly simmers just below his carefully controlled exterior. I rarely get angry.

Employees reach Jaunich via regular channels and must constantly anticipate his temper. Anyone can talk to me at any time, about anything—a freedom for which my managers criticized me more than once.

Jaunich makes decisions slowly and only after intense scrutiny, presumably on the grounds that decisions must be based on all obtainable facts. I make decisions quickly, since many "facts" turn out to be opinion, and not facts at all. I learned from my engineering days that it was pointless to include factors with only a one-percent effect on an answer—especially if I knew in advance that the answer was approximate anyway and unlikely to be within ten percent of the truth. There is much validity to the saying, "An accountant is someone who will give you a best estimate to five significant figures."

Jaunich was very reserved, very quiet, and operated from behind closed doors. I was gregarious and open, again perhaps to a fault.

While power and money did not motivate me, power seemed very important to Jaunich. He told me that money was one of his driving influences, agreeing with Jerry Sanders, founder of Advanced Micro Devices, who is alleged to have said that a man should be measured by how much money he has amassed. To me, that's one of the most incomprehensibly stupid measures of a man that anyone could propose.

But these differences were not, in my opinion, any basis for removing Jaunich just weeks after his arrival. Clearly he and I would never be personal friends, but his credentials for the position of Osborne Computer Corporation's CEO were far better than mine. So Jaunich remained, and I prepared myself for an early departure from the company.

During March and April of 1983 Jaunich did an excellent job recruiting competent new senior managers. In particular, it would be hard to find anyone who could match the excellence of John Hanne who left Texas Instruments in mid-April to join Osborne Computer Corporation as vice president of engineering. It was unfortunate that Jaunich did not recognize the value of some prior managers, Psaris in particular. As early as February Jaunich made it clear that Psaris had no place on his team. Frequently she was not even informed of meetings where, as vice president of sales and marketing, she should have been the one making decisions. But she, like me, was too exhausted to argue, so she also prepared for an earlier than expected departure.

Jaunich was running a high-flying company with a worldwide reputation. In early 1983, when traveling on company business I regularly met prime ministers and ambassadors (most of whom wanted stock in my company). I met the Crown Princess of Thailand (the King being sick), and I introduced Silicon Valley's leading entrepreneurs of English origin to Queen Elizabeth II when she visited San Francisco.

Osborne Computer Corporation's best quarter ever was the one ending February 1983. The company was production-bound through the end of the month. Dealers who had canceled January and February orders expecting a post-Christmas slowdown were pleading to have their orders reinstated. Table 13 shows the sales for these months compared to the 1983 budget figures prepared in 1982. The dip in January numbers reflects the manufacturing department's brief respite needed to recuperate from sheer exhaustion.

Table 13 **Osborne I shipments, December 1982–March 1983 (projected and actual).**

Month	*Projected*	*Actual*
December (1982)	6000	12633
January (1983)	6000	8290
February	7000	11785
March	7000	9914

But once again the heavy demand for product caused problems.

Following considerable internal argument and dissension, it was decided that Osborne I owners who wanted double density and eighty-column upgrades should bring their computers back to their local dealers who would ship them to the factory. We would then perform the upgrade in two days, and return the computers to the dealers. Owners would be without their computers for two weeks at the most.

Psaris and Osowick favored this approach on two grounds: the dealers did not want to perform upgrades, and we could handle the business profitably. I was against the plan because I had yet to see anything relating to engineering or hardware go smoothly, and smooth operations were a necessity if a two-day turnaround was to be even close to the mark. It was not.

The demand for computers was heavy through the end of February. Testology simply could not manufacture enough double density or eighty-column upgrade boards. Each day Fred Osowick, whose department was handling the upgrades, was told that "in two or three days" the problem would be solved. They were optimistic, but still the shortage remained. Osowick was finally given a few upgrade boards taken from the production line, which reduced the number of Osborne I's that could be built for shipment.

The trickle of upgrade boards was simply inadequate. Computers awaiting upgrade stacked up in the warehouse. By the time the inflow was shut off, the delay on some upgrades had stretched to five or six weeks. Meanwhile the owners of delayed computers were pestering their blameless dealers for a delivery date. As a result of this upgrade fiasco, a tremendous amount of ill will was generated between dealers and Osborne Computer Corporation.

Moreover, because of these problems, Osborne Computer Corporation took a huge loss on the upgrade program.

The eighty-column upgrade board caused even more problems. For no apparent reason, some microcomputers would not work after the eighty-column board had been added. In March of 1983 the company stopped performing eighty-column upgrades while the problem was investigated. It turned out to be an obscure incompatibility between chips used in the eighty-column upgrade and one particular brand of chip used in the main logic board during 1981 and early 1982. Some microcomputers that by chance had the wrong brand of chip on the main logic board would not work following the upgrade; others would.

Jaunich was an observer of the upgrade problems. He must have wondered about the whole quality control mechanism at this point.

In January of 1983 it became clear that the engineering and programming staff could not continue simultaneous development of both the Executive and the Vixen. To meet the April 17 introduction deadline, one of them would have to be placed on the back burner. I made the decision to emphasize the Executive at the expense of the Vixen. It was the last significant management decision I made before Jaunich took complete charge of the company. The Executive was the obvious choice: the first samples of the Vixen's plastic case were unavailable until April, so the Vixen would have to be delayed until May or June anyway. Moreover, the Vixen's design still included a five-inch monitor. We were all very sensitive by then to the negative perception this small screen had in the marketplace, and Al Stone had demonstrated that a seven-inch display would fit into the Vixen case, but Ed Richter assured me that it was not possible and claimed he had calculations to prove it. Al Stone was not one to bother with calculations, however; he built a unit and the argument was over.

Including the larger display units would delay the Vixen's introduction by an additional three or four months, but that seemed a small amount of time given the overwhelming advantages of the larger display.

To heal dealer relations, Jaunich asked Psaris to turn the Executive's introduction into a lavish, one-week whistle-stop tour around the country, during which dealers would be feted with food, drink, and product demonstrations. The tour began in San Jose, California, on Sunday, April 17, and ended in New York on the following Friday, April 22nd. Ninety-five percent of Osborne's dealers attended this celebration—an incredible response. Numerous magazine and newspaper articles appeared during this week that described the Executive in glowing terms. It was Psaris' last significant contribution to the company.

Unfortunately, the advertising campaign supporting the Executive's introduction was weak and ineffective because Jaunich, unimpressed with David Carlick's work, vetoed most of it without having any ready substitute. Seeing the writing on the wall, Carlick quit with no ill feelings: his heart was no longer in the work he did for Osborne Computer Corporation. Carlick felt all along that the Vixen should have been emphasized since it more closely reflected the early marketing theories developed by him and me—to make things cheaper and smaller and to offer more value. For Carlick the Executive was a step in the wrong direction.

The company was now without an advertising agency, and time was of the essence.

It was June before Jaunich replaced David Carlick with TKL, a Chicago-based agency. He paid them an $80,000-per-month retainer, while Carlick's average monthly bill to Osborne had been $10,000. For their fee TKL produced nothing until August, a few weeks before the company declared bankruptcy.

To meet a mid-April introduction, the company expected to start building Executives in mid-March so that by April 17 several thousand Executives would be sitting in the warehouse waiting to be shipped. But arguments over product reliability caused the Executives to be built, tested, and then rebuilt through the entire month of April.

Executive product reliability arguments centered on testing standards. Many units were failing quality assurance because of a few "soft" disk errors (as few as one soft disk error per million disk accesses). "Soft" disk errors occur when the disk drive requires two or more attempts to perform an operation before the operation is completed successfully. A user would see a slight slow-down in the computer's operating speed, but that would be the extent of it.

Knowing that shipments are critical to cash flow and profits, I favored shipping units that had been rejected solely on the basis of soft errors. True, we would have to hunt down the cause of these errors, but that could be done later. Jaunich disagreed. All units were to be rebuilt until a sufficiently high percentage of them passed all quality control tests, including the soft error test.

At the time it appeared to me as though Jaunich was being pig-headed and highly irresponsible about the whole matter. I was no longer in touch with the company's financial condition, as I had been when I was running the company; yet I could not understand the chances Jaunich appeared to be taking with the company's survival. Dan Costa, director of quality assurance, sided with Jaunich. This did not impress me; most quality assurance managers will "cover their ass" by setting testing standards so high that little if any product ever gets shipped.

I made my last attempt at the Oakland Airport to talk Jaunich into shipping Executives. His temper took over. In front of Psaris (and much to her embarrassment), Jaunich screamed that there was no way he would ship any machines.

I backed down. Psaris had never seen me act that way before. She made up her mind to quit. That same day I also decided to leave. The company mood had grown somber and tense. If to find out what was going on I had to risk Jaunich's temper to get behind his closed door, what chance did any lesser mortal have? In the absence of information, which in the past had flowed so freely, the company was now riddled with rumors and innuendo; the first simmerings of discontent were beginning to appear. Working at Osborne Computer Corporation was no fun anymore. I still had no reason to distrust the man I personally had recruited to take my job, so the choice appeared as stark as it was plain: ask the Board to remove Jaunich because he and I disagreed, or leave myself.

John Hanne joined the company at the end of April as vice president of engineering. Executives were shipped during the first week of May. Hanne made a couple of important changes that turned the Executive into what must be the most reliable microcomputer on the market today. IBM never sought such reliability before it started shipping personal computers, and Osborne certainly could not afford that luxury.

Pricing also remained an issue right up to the Executive introduction, but on this issue I was almost alone. Only Joe Roebuck, recently hired from Apple as vice president of marketing, halfheartedly sided with me.

I was in favor of returning to the $1995 retail price initially proposed in early 1982. Everyone else suggested higher prices, ranging as high as $2695. Ultimately $2495—the price selected by the marketing department in late 1982—held. Based on the introductory week, this retail price appeared to be a good choice. Dealers ordered product enthusiastically; very few complained that the price was too high, and many approved it since they received a larger profit margin. We returned from the introductory tour with approximately $25 million worth of Executive orders.

Chapter Seven A PUBLIC OFFERING

With the surge in sales that came in late 1982 and the continuing volume of positive press, underwriters became even more insistent that it was time for Osborne Computer Corporation to have a public stock offering.

Anyone who has not experienced the persistence of America's underwriting firms cannot fully understand how persuasive these people are. When they decide that a company is a hot prospect for a public offering, you either go along and have a public offering, or you post guards to keep underwriters off your property.

Through the latter months of 1982, Osborne Computer Corporation was besieged by underwriters of every stripe attempting to participate in the public offering that they were determined to make happen. At the time I personally believed that the company was not ready for a public offering and the Board of Directors concurred. Nevertheless, each week chief executive officers from America's most prestigious underwriting firms would personally call me or Ottinger to make their case.

They insisted it was not necessary for a hypergrowth company to show profits before going public. Of course hypergrowth companies operate from crisis to crisis, they warbled reassuringly.

A break finally came when Ottinger attended an American Electronics Association conference in Florida. He was so overwhelmed by the insistence of every underwriter he met that he came back a converted man. Before long the Board and I were also swayed. None of us had looked upon Osborne Computer Corporation as a device for getting rich quick via a public offering, as so many start-up companies appear to do, but the multimillion-dollar war chests acquired by competitors via public offerings could not be ignored. Without equivalent financial resources we could easily find ourselves fighting money with ingenuity. And the money would win.

The end-of-November annual statement (shown in Table 14) certainly looked as though it would generate an excellent public offering. One persuasive argument was that Altos had already gone public with spectacular success, although in the opinion of both Osborne's management and Board, Altos was actually a less viable candidate for a public offering.

Table 14 **Income statement year end November 27, 1982.**

Osborne Computer Corporation
Consolidated Statement of Operations

	Year End Nov. 27, 1982	Year End Nov. 28, 1981	Year End Nov. 29, 1980
Net sales	$68,783,000	$5,761,000	$ —
Costs and expenses:			
Cost of sales	50,795,000	3,878,000	—
R & D (including initial production costs in 1981)	1,643,000	1,282,000	28,000
Marketing	12,745,000	960,000	—
General & admin.	3,531,000	832,000	9,000
Total Costs and expenses	68,714,000	6,952,000	37,000
Operating income (loss)	69,000	(1,191,000)	(37,000)
Interest expense	1,090,000	91,000	—
Net loss	$(1,021,000)	$(1,282,000)	$(37,000)
Net loss per common share	$ (.39)	$ (.83)	$ (.10)
Common shares used in computing per-share amounts	2,601,710	1,541,009	378,560

Jaunich's arrival at Osborne Computer Corporation in January of 1983 coincided with the start of serious preparations for a public stock offering. Prior to Jaunich's arrival, Ottinger and the Board had decided to go ahead with the public offering, and had selected the most impressive team of underwriters they could find. If there was to be a public offering, it had to be the best. After much discussion, interviewing, and analyzing, Salomon Brothers was selected as the lead underwriter, supported by Rothschild Unterberg Towbin and Smith Barney.

In my opinion the underwriter selection process was a meaningless social minuet, important only to the most rarified strata of the financial community. The country seemed to be suffering from Osborne stock fever at that time. If Osborne Computer Corporation had had a public stock offering during the first quarter of 1983, it most certainly would have been sold out—whether handled by Wall Street's most pretigious underwriters or by firms at the other end of the spectrum. In either case a public stock offering would have turned into an old-fashioned buying frenzy.

But both the Board and Jim Ottinger wanted only the best. To them that meant Salomon Brothers or Goldman Sachs as the lead underwriter, supported by one high-tech underwriter and a good retail operation. Why not?

Preliminary meetings between Osborne management and representatives of the underwriters began in early January. The plan was to schedule a public offering for the first week of March. But after conducting due diligence interviews, the underwriters issued an opinion that the time was not in fact right for a public offering. The cited four reasons as I recall them (I no longer have a copy of the memo) are summarized as follows:

1. The transition to a new management team was incomplete.
2. Two new products were to be introduced and there might be delays in the introduction.
3. The company's future success depended on how well the new products did.
4. There was continuing instability in financial forecasts for the current quarter and future quarters.

A postponement of the company's public offering did not appear to be a setback. Preliminary December numbers and back order levels suggested that the current quarter would be the company's best ever.

The only hint that trouble might exist anywhere on the horizon occurred in December of 1982. After sending representatives to visit with

Jim Ottinger, the Bank of America (then Osborne Computer Corporation's bank) refused to extend the company's line of credit above the $10-million level that had been in effect for almost a year. The bank claimed their decision was based on a corporate policy of reducing their level of high-tech business and in no way reflected negatively on Osborne Computer Corporation. Nevertheless Osborne management considered it a very disagreeable act on the part of the bank. After all, the company had grown enormously in a year: if it was good for a $10-million line of credit in January 1982, surely it should be good for more a year later, especially given the company's growth.

But no. Ten million dollars was as far as the Bank of America would go. They relented a little, allowing an additional $5-million short-term loan, good until the end of January, by which time the company had to find other sources of funds. It did. Ottinger negotiated a $20-million line of credit with Security Pacific Bank, who in turn passed on part of the loan to Chemical Bank of New York and to National Westminster Bank as secondary participants.

There was no reason to question the Bank of America's reasons for demurring at the time. A curious incident suggests that they may have arrived at a very negative conclusion after visiting Ottinger and reviewing our financial condition, which may explain why they refused to increase the company's bank debt. In April of 1983 one of our programmers came to see me at home late at night. He arrived with his girlfriend. Both were very nervous.

"I think you should hear what Cindy has to say," the agitated programmer said. ("Cindy" is a fictitious name.) "She knows a guy who says Osborne will never go public and my stock will never be worth anything, so not to count on it."

No bombshells had yet struck the company, so I was merely curious. "Tell me about Cindy's friend," I replied.

Cindy's friend had a very wealthy father who apparently was trying to interest the boy in the world of business and high finance. Accordingly, Cindy's friend had accompanied his father to some high-level meetings with senior Bank of America executives. The gist of discussions at these meetings was that Osborne Computer Corporation was in trouble, was unlikely to go public, and would probably not survive the year.

"We think it's a Kaypro conspiracy to get at you personally and at the company in general," the programmer told me. "Mr. Kay really hates you personally and wants to get you."

"Kaypro? What do they have to do with it?" I asked.

According to Cindy, her friend's father had some type of financial link with Kaypro, a major Osborne competitor.

I dismissed the entire story. The only corroborative evidence that Cindy could produce was a cassette tape on which her friend spoke vaguely about things he had heard said at the Bank of America meeting. Nothing on the tape incriminated Kaypro. Nor was there any evidence that Kaypro would stoop to unethical behavior.

But in my opinion the Bank of America meeting almost certainly did occur, probably in March of 1983. There was no way Cindy could have known as much as she did about circumstances surrounding Osborne's change in bankers without the information coming from a very knowledgeable source. However, in recent conversations with Cindy, she had a very different and far more innocent tale to tell. This may reflect her fear of becoming involved in current litigation, and dragging her friend in with her, or it may represent inaccurate recollections on my part. But if the meeting did occur, the disclosures made by senior Bank of America officials could prove quite exciting should they be verified in court.

I did not make any connection at the time. In retrospect I believe that senior bank officials might have told Cindy's friend's father about their negative findings at Osborne the previous December.

The postponement of the March public offering adversely affected my personal finances, which were stretched to the limit. Recently married and having just rebuilt a lush Berkeley Hills home, I needed money to complete the reconstruction and for income taxes in April. The solution was to sell some company shares in advance of the public offering. I initially intended to sell only a few shares; however, as February rolled by and it became apparent that Jaunich and I would not get along, I decided to hedge my bets and sell enough shares to keep the wolf from the door. So I sold $1,500,000 worth of shares to Robert Bily, a member of the Board of Directors and also a member of the Board's audit committee. Bily was aware of the risks, after attending an audit committee meeting with Les Hogan and Arthur Young representatives to review the 1982 audited year-end statement.

The shares Robert Bily bought represented approximately ten percent of my holdings in Osborne Computer Corporation at that time. As a favor, I also agreed to sell shares to certain distributors and friends who had persisted in their requesting some stock. These additional transactions were never completed.

Given the voracious appetite for money that accompanies any hypergrowth situation, Osborne Computer Corporation found itself again running short of funds in mid-February. Executive inventory had to be purchased, and there was barely enough cash to keep up with the Osborne I. We could still borrow from Security Pacific Bank, but only if the borrowing level was secured by sufficient accounts receivable and inventory collateral. It became clear that the collateral would be insufficient to meet the company's borrowing needs between February and the time a public offering would occur.

At the suggestion of a representative from one of the underwriters, Ottinger recommended that we bridge the gap by getting investors to guarantee the difference. This was done by obtaining letters of credit from investors to cover the difference between the company's borrowing needs and its collateral base. These letters of credit carried with them warrants to purchase stock at what was then thought to be a favorable price. Each letter-of-credit holder would be allowed to buy Osborne stock worth ten percent of his letter-of-credit amount, paying $50 per share. At that time the shares were thought to be worth between $80 and $100 per share on a public offering basis. Of course, prior to a public offering Osborne shares would be split to yield an offering price of $15 to $20 per share, the popular price for prestigious new issues.

New management and new product introductions seemed like good reasons for conservative underwriters to recommend postponing a public stock offering. There were also valid financial reasons for the underwriters to issue their postponement opinion.

Ottinger uncovered errors in the financial statement for the quarter ending February 1983 that might require restating numbers for the fiscal year ending November 1982. Arthur Young, the company's auditors, were asked to return and examine these inconsistencies. (It is my perception that auditors do not like admitting that their audited statements contain errors. It is a very professional, macho thing with them. In my opinion, they would far prefer to conclude that errors, when found, all belonged to the time period just following their audit.) In the end a confrontation with Arthur Young was avoided by changing the fiscal year-end from November to February. I personally have no basis for reaching any conclusions as to whether this move was, or was not, justified. I simply lack the expertise to comment, and I did not personally participate in these discussions. However, it does appear to me that this new year end in no way changed the total picture for the year; it merely avoided a battle between the company and the auditors as to whether the errors belonged to the year ending November, which Arthur Young had audited, or whether the mistakes occurred in December, January, and February—which they had not.

One might assume that by early April problems hindering a public stock offering would be resolved. On April 6, Jaunich sent all stockholders the following letter:

OSBORNE COMPUTER CORPORATION
April 6, 1983
Dear Investor:
We have now received commitments in excess of $9.0 million for the bridge financing and are prepared to close the transaction.
During the period of placement activity, several events have occurred. We believe it appropriate that you be aware of these prior to the formal closing.
First, we have hired several key executives. Our new Vice President of Marketing, Joseph Roebuck, joins us from Apple Computer, where he was a Director of Marketing. Prior to that, he was with Honeywell for about seventeen years. A new Chief Financial Officer, Donald Waite, has joined us from Measurex, where he held a similar position. Earlier, he was Chief Financial Officer both at Memorex and Bell and Howell, where he was employed for about twelve years. James Ottinger, previously Chief Financial Officer, has become Vice President and General Manager of Osborne's North American profit center. H. "Bert" Carson has joined us as Vice President of Human Resources. He previously held this position with Microdata Corp. and Coca-Cola Bottling Company of Los Angeles. Earlier in his career, Bert spent about fifteen years serving in the various human resource functions at General Electric Corp.
Second, a new product, the first in what we are calling the Executive Series, is scheduled for introduction within two weeks in a series of meetings with dealers around the country. At these meetings, we will give each dealer a demonstration product to take with him. Thus, we are announcing a product which will be commercially available in limited shipping quantities immediately following the announcement. The Executive will be priced at about $2500. Harris Corporation has agreed to be a nationwide dealer for this product, and the Company expects sales to large institutions and customers not covered in our normal distribution network.
Third, during the past few days, we have conducted a thorough review with our lawyers and investment bankers and we are now mov-

ing ahead with preparations for a public offering. Based on the current schedule, the Company plans to file within the next six weeks.

We believe the Company valuation eventually determined by the underwriters and the Company will be based on a combination of quantitative and qualitative factors, including the results of our financial forecasts.

Fourth, we have decided to change our accounting year to a February year-end from a November year-end. Our auditors, Arthur Young & Company, will have audited year-end results for the two previous fiscal years on this new basis in time for inclusion in a registration statement. There are several reasons for the change and its timing. Most importantly, the change allows the Company to focus on sales and customer support during the peak holiday period. It also facilitates the closing of the Company's books at a more convenient time of year. By making the change before becoming a public company, we make easier communications with analysts and others who normally deal in year-to-year and quarter-to-quarter comparisons.

In changing the fiscal year, new results will show the Company had fiscal year revenues in excess of $94.0 million versus $68.7 million in the previously reported fiscal year ending November 27, 1982. The Company will still report a loss in excess of $1.0 million for the most recent year ended February 26, 1983.

Preliminary results for the quarter ending February 26, 1983 indicate revenues of approximately $34.0 million and profits at approximately breakeven. This represents a shortfall in profit. Some of this reflects expense items not included in the annual budget. These are being addressed in our revised projections. Other expense items are basically of a nonrecurring nature and relate to the start-up of our east coast manufacturing facility and build-up of international operations. To certify financial statements for the year ended February 26, 1983, an audit is now being conducted by Arthur Young & Company.

We are now reviewing the financial plan for the fiscal year ending in February 1984, a period during which we expect a high level of new product activity and improved operating results. In sum, we are encouraged that progress is being made and the outlook for profitability is good.

Sincerely,

Robert Jaunich
President and
Chief Executive Officer

Between April 8 and April 14 letters of credit backing $8,400,000 were obtained from shareholders enabling the company to borrow additional funds from its banks. Obtaining the letters of credit had not been easy. The venture capital community offered a less-than-enthusiastic response. They would have been happy to buy additional shares but did not understand why they should be backing loans. So the letter-of-credit terms were sweetened to carry with them the right to buy Osborne stock worth twenty percent of the letter-of-credit amount, at $40 per share. In mid-March Jerry Petruzzelli, the company's attorney, advised me that to set a good example I should also become a letter-of-credit holder. Knowing nothing about letters of credit, I discussed the matter with my banker and then insured a $1-million letter of credit.

The company's public offering was now rescheduled for the first week of June.

Waiting at an airport midway through the Executive introduction tour, Jaunich updated me on the latest financial figures. I had just returned from Japan and was out of touch.

"It looks as though the February numbers have settled down," he said. "The year's loss will be somewhere between $1 and 4 million." I asked Dennis Bovin of Salomon Brothers if that would impact the public offering. He thought not. They would lower the offering price. "I think we should leave the loss at $4 million," he concluded.

"What about this quarter?" I asked Jaunich. "We haven't shipped much this month."

"We'll probably break even," Jaunich replied. "But the cash situation could be a problem. Don (Waite) says we'll be out of cash by the last week of May. If we get the offering money in the second week of June—that shouldn't be a problem though."

On the morning of Friday, April 22, the last day of the Executive introductory tour, Ottinger, Jaunich, and I met with representatives of the underwriters, including Dennis Bovin, at the Hyatt-Grand Central Hotel in New York City. Jaunich told the underwriters that the company would report a loss of approximately $4 million on a $100-million net for a restated fiscal year ending February 1983.

The underwriters agreed that a $4-million loss was not objectionable. They restated what underwriters had said before: that strong earnings were not necessary during the early, very high-growth period of a new company. The offering price would be lowered, but the public stock offering was on. They would visit the company the following week to complete their final due diligence. Then the company's intention to go public would be announced.

The following Monday I left for Golden, Colorado, to visit the Adolph Coors Brewing Company where I was scheduled to give a seminar. That Tuesday night I received a telephone call from Jaunich.

"Adam, this is Bob," Jaunich began, in his usual precise and flat tone. "Unfortunately, as chief executive officer it is my duty to inform you that over the weekend Don uncovered considerable additional losses."

"Additional losses?" I asked. "But just last Friday you said the loss would be $4 million for the year ending February, and a breakeven current quarter."

"The losses will be much greater than that," Jaunich replied in his monotone.

"How great?" I asked.

"It looks like between $8 and 10 million for the year ending February, with another $10 million for the current quarter."

My head swam. "That's not possible," I replied.

For Osborne Computer Corporation it was the beginning of the end.

There is no question that a public offering would have saved Osborne Computer Corporation. The question then is whether the law surrounding start-up company public stock offerings is equitable. In my opinion, the answer is no. As one would expect, the law strongly favors the people who have a lot of money, at the expense of people who do not.

Investing in a company when it goes public is almost as risky as investing in that same company when it is a start-up, being funded only by venture capital. And yet a company's shares increase most dramatically directly before the public offering. Public offerings are supposed to give companies a secure financial base for future growth. Too often the principal goal of a public offering is to let the early investors get rich quick. That being the case, it is high time the public was allowed to play the venture capital game. There should be more venture capital funds open to the average small investor, and securities regulations should make it easier for such funds to exist and to operate.

A QUESTION OF SECURITIES LAW

A hard question that must be asked then is, are public offerings being used properly by high-technology start-up companies, or is there need for reform?

Table 15 provides statistics for a number of high-technology companies that have had recent public offerings. This table shows the financial result upon which the company went public, the offering price for the company's shares, and the value that this offering price assigned to the company. The table also shows what happened subsequently to the company's performance and stock-price fluctuations.

Despite any rules of the Securities and Exchange Commission or any other government agency, it is essentially impossible for any numbers to truly reflect the condition of a start-up company that is about to go public. Prior to a public offering, many of these companies are propelled forward by a few driven individuals with stars and dollar-signs in their eyes. After the public offering, bureaucracy normally sets in, and the human productivity reflected in a statement prior to a public offering becomes fiction within the new, post-public-offering reality. Even the financial statements themselves must be taken with a pinch of salt. If mature companies play the game of seeing what they can get past their auditors—and many do—then even with the best of intentions, an auditing firm has little hope of truly representing any start-up company's condition, given the fluidity and dynamics of high growth.

Published financial results of a company about to go public can give broad indications of its operating habits and financial condition. For example, Kaypro achieved profitability by spending little or nothing on advertising and marketing. This is obvious, and investors can make their own judgements accordingly. But marginal profits or losses reported by companies are indicative of nothing. There are too many variables beyond an accountant's grasp that allow any group of managers to manipulate expenses by a few percentage points, legitimately and within the law.

The real basis upon which anyone should invest in a start-up is whether the company is in a market where a lot of participants have significant growth potential. This was not the case for the microcomputer industry once IBM entered the fray. Not even Apple Computer Corporation's stock has been able to perform well in the years since it went public, simply because IBM soaked up such a large overall part of the market. Few if any microcomputer hardware manufacturers offer attractive long-term investment opportunities. The attractive opportunities lie elsewhere, in industries where there never has been a single dominant force. Computer software is an example. The closest analogy to software publishing and distribution is the book publishing industry, which has never been able to sustain a dominant giant since taste and personal opinion have so much to do with sales choices. When the price ticket is low, buyers tend to be more capricious. When the price is high, security drives them to follow the herd. Computer supplies offers substantial opportunities. In other words, IBM (and in all probability AT&T) will dominate the razor business. Investors should seek their opportunities in razor blades.

Insofar as public offerings themselves are concerned, industry in America operates according to the law. Altruism as an operating principle tends to generate less-favorable financial results. Based on this premise, it is the duty of any emerging high-tech company to seek a public offering at the time most appropriate for its welfare, following the law and disclosing facts fully. Then it is up to potential investors to examine the disclosed facts and determine whether the risk is worth taking.

On this premise Osborne Computer Corporation could have and should have gone public in March of 1983. Disclosure statements should have pointed out the risks associated with the introduction of new products, the transition to a new management team, and the unreliability of financial data in any company growing as fast as Osborne was growing. This would have served the interests of the company and its stockholders. The company could not have gone public in April, based on the facts as Jaunich reported them. If properly described in a disclosure document, these facts would have alarmed the community sufficiently to send Osborne Computer Corporation to an early grave. And without disclosing everything that was known about the company's circumstances, the offering would have been illegal.

Osborne's management did continue to examine the viability of a public offering. As late as August of 1983 I was amazed to discover that Jaunich was actively exploring a public offering, even though it was clear that bankruptcy was just weeks away. Jaunich told me that he had contacted Rooney Pace and D. H. Blair to see if they would consider taking the company public as a last-minute rescue from bankruptcy. One of the underwriters had contacted Bateman, Eichler, Hill, Richards on behalf of the company. And given the law, as it is written, Jaunich was probably acting correctly in attempting this move. As chief executive officer of the company he was obliged to do everything in his power to prevent a bankruptcy.

Table 15 **Industry data on public offerings of high-technology companies.**

Company Name	Date of Initial Offering	Underwriter	Initial Price	Number of Shares Initially Offered	Net Proceeds Received from Init. Offering	Quarterly Earnings Per share			Average Number of Shares Currently Outstanding	Price per Share May 1, 1984
Alpha Microsystems	June 18, 1981	Led by Bateman Eichler, Hill, Richards Inc.	$15.00	975,000 (815,000 represent new financing	$12,225,000	 May Aug. Nov. Feb. Total	1983–84 .28 .32 .35	1982–83 .01 .20 .18 .24 .63	2,888,421 common Jan. 23, 1984	$15.00
Altos Computer System	Nov. 4, 1982	Led by LF Rothschild, Unterberg, Towbin and Robertson, Colman, Stephens & Woodman	$21.00	3,630,000 (3,030,000 represent new financing)	$58,830,000	 Sep. Dec. Mar. Jun. Total	1983–84 .08	1982–83 .16 .11 .16 .15 .58	13,655,172 common Dec. 14, 1983	$9.75
Apple Computer	Dec. 12, 1980	Led by Morgan Stanley & Co. and Hambrecht & Quist	$22.00	4,600,000 (4,000,000 represent new financing)	$88,000,000	 Dec. Mar. Jun. Sep. Total	1982–83 .40 .40 .40 .03 1.28	1981–82 .24 .24 .26 .32 1.06	59,867,000 common Oct. 21, 1983	$31.38
COMPAQ Computer	Dec. 9, 1983	Led by LF Rothschild, Unterberg, Towbin and EF Hutton & Co. Inc.	$11.00	6,000,000	$66,000,000	 Mar. Jun. Sep. Dec.		1983 d0.85 d0.33 0.10	3,735,000 common Jan. 16, 1984	$6.75

Company Name	Date of Initial Offering	Underwriter	Initial Price	Number of Shares Initially Offered	Net Proceeds Received from Init. Offering	Quarterly Earnings Per share			Average Number of Shares Currently Outstanding	Price per Share May 1, 1984
Fortune Systems	Mar. 4, 1983	Led by First Boston Corp.; Alex. Brown & Sons and Montgomery Securities	$22.00	5,000,000 (4,400,000 represent new financing)	$96,800,000		1983	1982	17,257,000 common July 13, 1983	$3.63
						Mar.	.10	d0.14		
						Jun.		d0.19		
						Sep.		d0.05		
						Dec.		0.16		
						Total		d0.19		
Kaypro Corporation	Aug. 25, 1983	Led by Prudential-Bache Securities	$10.00	4,000,000 (3,000,000 represent new financing)	$30,000,000		1982–83	1981–82	33,219,000 common Oct. 14, 1983	$6.50
						Nov.	—	—		
						Feb.	a0.13	d0.01		
						May	b0.08	NM		
						Aug.				
						Total		d0.01		
Victor Technologies	March 23, 1983	Led by LF Rothschild, Unterberg, Towbin; Bear, Stearns & Co. and Charterhouse Japhet plc.	$17.50	4,500,000 (2,000,000 represent new financing)	$35,000,000		1983	1982	999,585 common Oct. 14, 1983	q $1.25 Entered Chapter 11 Late February 1984
						Mar.	d0.34	d1.58		
						Jun.	d0.66	d0.72		
						Sep.		d1.04		
						Dec.		.93		
						Total		d2.41		

d=Deficit
a=6 months
b=2 months end April
NM=Not meaningful
q=In bankruptcy proceedings

Sources: Standard and Poore's Financial Data
Form 10-K from Altos
Annual report and form 10-K from Apple
Wall Street Journal

Chapter Eight COLLAPSE

During the week of the Executive introduction tour in April of 1983, Fred Brown (by then vice president of sales) realized the magnitude of the Osborne I problems facing the company. Some fifteen thousand Osborne I's—nearly all of them double density—were in finished goods or parts inventory, waiting to be sold into a dealer network already choking with unsold machines. Osborne I sales had collapsed following the end of the free dBASEII offer in February, as Figure 2 in Chapter 9 illustrates. On his own initiative Fred Brown stayed in New York after the Executive introduction and made two deals to sell off excess Osborne I inventory. One was with Bob Leviton, a well-known surplus goods dealer, who wanted to buy four to six thousand Osborne I's for $980 each. The other was with Trans World Airlines, who would advertise the Osborne I at a special discount to their frequent fliers, offering them units for $1495 each, with a 20,000-mile frequent flier bonus for each buyer.

According to Fred Brown, Jaunich's reaction lacked enthusiasm. Instead of finding a way to consummate quick sales, Jaunich asked Waite, Ottinger, and Roebuck for opinions and statistics. By the end of May, Fred Brown's two deals were dead. In Brown's opinion they died in consequence of endless indecision and inactivity, both impossible constraints when disposing of a dead product line's remainders, especially in an environment where the product's realizable value can decline sharply within a week. Shortly thereafter Fred Brown resigned, claiming the company was being "set up." At the time Brown was the only employee to feel this way. But in his words, "Any attempt I made to sell inventory was vetoed or tabled to die of old age. I had better things to do with my time."

Fred Brown further complained, "Jaunich kept calling me at home in the evening to ask if I was part of his team, if I was willing to risk my house, when all I really wanted to do was sell product."

Arguments surrounding Fred Brown's deals generally dealt with the issue of dealer-price protection, which Brown said could be circumvented, though others disagreed. Dealer-price protection might have committed the company to reducing the price of all unsold Osborne I computers that had been bought in the previous sixty days and remained unsold.

After calling me on Tuesday, April 26, to report the company's sharply deteriorating financial condition, Jaunich canceled the underwriters' due diligence trip and informed the banks that the Osborne Computer Corporation was no longer in compliance with its loan provisions. He also reported that according to Waite's calculations the company would be out of cash by the second week of May. With no public offering on the horizon and the company in trouble with the banks, the situation was desperate.

An emergency Board of Directors meeting was held on the morning of Friday, April 29. A somber group gathered in the Board room exchanging gallows humor while Don Waite described the losses for the fiscal year ending February 1983, together with the additional losses he would report for the subsequent quarter. These losses are summarized in Table 18.

"And in case you think that you've heard the worst of the bad news," he said after describing a particularly bleak set of revised reserve accounts, "let me show you this." And he produced new charts to highlight the current quarter's financial disasters.

Here are highlights of the April 29 Board meeting:

1. Jaunich claimed he had no knowledge of possible poorer financial data until April 21.
2. Jaunich observed that the death of the Osborne I had occured faster than anyone could have predicted.
3. Dennis Bovin of Salomon Brothers, on behalf of the underwriters, stated that they would work with the company to raise money providing top management remained and no evidence of fraud or misrepresentation was found.

But the picture was not uniformly bleak. The company had come back from its Executive introductory road show with orders in hand for approximately $25-million worth of Executives to be shipped in the next ninety days. The company was once again production-bound; it could not build enough computers to meet dealer demand. This situation remained until mid-June. In fact, the domestic demand for Executives was so heavy that international introductions were postponed until September.

The underwriters advised the company to slash costs and to obtain interim financing at once and by any means available. A public offering would follow at such time as the company had regained its financial health. Waite estimated that the company would need between $20 and $30 million to tide it over until a public offering brought in additional funds, presumably in early 1984. The underwriters thought this sum could probably be raised via a private placement of stock selling at between $6 and $12 a share, down sharply from the valuations ranging between $60 and $100 a share that had been discussed earlier in the year.

The underwriters made it clear that they were staying with the company only because of Jaunich's presence and the presence of Jaunich's new management team. Over dinner Dennis Bovin of Salomon Brothers made the point with stark clarity: "Of course, without the new management team the company is dead," he said.

Board meetings were called in quick succession. The next one was on Thursday May 5. Here are the highlights:

1. Waite explained that the company was already in trouble with suppliers, many of whom were making deliveries only with cash in advance. Moreover, the company would need $4 million for cash flow the next week, none of which could come from bank borrowing. In fact, the company needed $4 million of new equity immediately. $30 million would be needed in the long term.
2. The Board tried to establish a value for the company but failed.
3. The Board resolved that management (Jaunich) should proceed immediately to try to raise $30 million of new equity.

At the investors meeting that followed the May 5 Board meeting, representatives of the venture capital community stated that raising the required $30 million of new equity would not be difficult. Per-share prices ranging between $6 and $15 were suggested. One representative from a venture capital firm (I cannot recall which) stated that in his opinion $30 million could be raised immediately at a price of approximately $15 per share, providing the underwriting was handled by a company such as Hambrecht and Quest—a company with extensive experience in this type of private offering. During this meeting the underwriters reiterated that Jaunich's continued presence was imperative to the company's survival.

Jaunich concluded the meeting by noting that his continued presence depended on a new compensation package that had not yet been negotiated with the Board.

Since late April Les Hogan and Jack Melchor had been questioning Bob Jaunich's motives based on their observation that Jaunich was making strange decisions where he was making any decisions at all. Following the May 5 investors' meeting I met with Melchor and Hogan in the parking lot.

"The company's being set up," Hogan insisted.

"It's certainly getting no leadership," Melchor agreed. "I was amazed at Bob stating in front of all those people that they couldn't count on his staying with the company. He just about killed any chance of raising any money with that statement."

"I think we should get rid of him and come in ourselves," Hogan said emphatically.

Melchor and Hogan were ready to fire Jaunich and run the company themselves until the crisis was over. It was I who dissuaded them. I had heard Dennis Bovin once too often stress that Salomon Brothers were prepared to handle a private placement providing Jaunich was running the company. If Jaunich was fired and the underwriters walked away could Melchor and Hogan raise $30 million? And would Waite stay? Or Hanne? I felt that these were imprudent risks to be taking at such a time of crisis.

Jaunich must have gotten wind of Hogan and Melchor's statements. The next morning he burst into my office fuming.

"There is talk that I am not playing from a full deck," he told me. "If anyone feels that way about me, I am prepared to resign right now."

"That is about the same as not reaching an agreement for your continued employment," I thought quietly. And I kept the thought to myself. Instead I smoothed trouble waters, persuading everyone that Jaunich should remain.

But there was a more immediate problem. Jaunich and Waite reported that Security Pacific Bank had taken a very hard line with the company. They were not prepared to extend the company any more credit. They expected the company to bring in more equity, and to do so quickly, or they would call the existing loans.

At that time Osborne Computer Corporation's total equity base was less than $13 million. Bank officials might be excused for believing that this equity base was woefully insufficient for a company that in two years had gone from nothing to more than $10 million a month in sales and was now seeking an extension in a $20-million bank line of credit.

Melchor immediately raised about $12 million in new equity, nearly all of it coming from the existing venture capital investors. New Series B Preferred shares were issued to these investors. Even I invested $160,000 in B Preferred shares, initially on behalf of a trust for two of my nieces, although I eventually absorbed the investment myself.

On May 13, ninety-two people were laid off. Of these approximately eighty were temporaries. The remainder really were for the most part poor performers with little future in the company. Nearly half of the international work force was terminated in advance of the May 13 Hayward layoff. June 16 saw the second layoff. Ninety-three people were terminated, but once again the bulk of them were temporaries. Nevertheless, the press swarmed around the company looking for a story.

Later Jack Dulaney of Smith Barney was to severely criticize Jaunich for being so timid in his cost cutting, but at that time no one acted as though they thought the company's problems would last for long.

The next Board meeting was on May 25. The following significant events occurred:

1. Seymour Rubinstein resigned from the Board citing conflicts of interest.
2. Waite stated that he still did not have final numbers for either the February or the May quarters, but that the company's cash needs remained critical.
3. Waite said the company needed $30 million in new equity as quickly as possible.
4. Waite suggested changing the fiscal year to end in May so that all losses could be swept into this past time period.
5. The B Preferred shares closing was discussed. May 27 was the scheduled closing date.
6. Melchor noted that the company still had not reached agreement with Jaunich on a new employment contract and could not proceed with the Series B Preferred stock sale until such a contract had been agreed to. Jaunich agreed to the terms of a new contract that day, but the agreement meant very little; it was the first of many.

The Series B Preferred stock closed on Friday, May 27, after hanging on a knife's edge for the better part of two weeks. Before releasing these funds Melchor wanted to be as sure as possible that the rest of the financing would occur via a timely sale of Series C Preferred stock.

Meanwhile, through the end of May and into early June, auditors from Arthur Anderson interviewed members of Osborne's management on behalf of the Board's audit committee, looking for any illegalities associated with the company's alarming change in fortunes. They found none, and so stated in their final report.

Still the continuing bad news was broken by occasional rays of sunshine. The optimism that had run so deeply throughout the early days began to emerge again. Osborne Computer Corporation was down but not out. There were problems, but they could be solved. The company employees believed it, management believed it, and the investors believed it.

I spent a lot of time visiting user groups and making special appearances at dealerships around the country, all in an effort to boost sales and keep morale high. However, I also used these trips to gather data that would support price reductions for both the Osborne I and the Executive.

But there were still clouds on the horizon. I had been keeping in close touch with dealers and was beginning to hear fairly uniform reports that Executives were moving slowly out of showrooms. Tad Kruzeweics of the Computique chain in Los Angeles and representatives of the Digital Deli in Mountain View were the first to warn me of this development. I now believed that the proper retail price for the Osborne I had fallen to $1295. I was still convinced that the proper price for the Executive was $1995. In support of this, selected computer store chains were to offer special short-term sales at this price. There was a dramatic increase in sales. More than three times as many computers were sold as compared to the $2495 price.

Jaunich argued that the Executive price could not be reduced from $2495 because it was simply too expensive to manufacture. I responded that Jaunich was basing this argument on the cost of goods computed for the first month of the Executive's manufacture and that was no basis for long-term pricing.

Jaunich presented two additional arguments for not reducing the price of the Osborne I or the Executive. The first was the money that would be lost through dealer price protection. The second was that the banks were already nervous. They would become more nervous when faced with the large reduction in accounts receivable that would accompany any price protection given to dealers for inventory that was less than ninety days old, the time for which the company was committed to making new dealer prices retroactive.

I felt that dealer price protection was a bullet the company would simply have to bite if it wanted to stay in business, which meant continuing to sell product at prices the market would accept.

As for the banks, they were not going to be delighted when faced with the dwindling sales levels that were inevitable given an overpriced and underpromoted product. At $2495 for the Executive and $1995 for the Osborne I, they may have stood a chance if supported by a barrage of highly positive publicity backed up with an excellent advertising campaign. By the summer of 1983, however, what publicity there was, was neutral at best. And the company was in an advertising hiatus following the departure of David Carlick.

By mid-June George Carr had put everyone on ten-hour shifts. Every Executive that could be built was being shipped, although international deliveries had not even begun. This gave people within the company a false sense of security. What the company saw in June was "pipe filling." Dealers were ordering inventory. But the inventory was not selling.

In the United Kingdom, for the months of May, June, and July, the Osborne I was the first- or second-best-selling microcomputer in the one thousand to two thousand-pound range, as reported by a microcomputer magazine survey. Mike Healy, president of Osborne U.K., was selling between 500 and 1000 computers a month.

With this good news, I left on a European goodwill tour aimed at getting positive press coverage prior to the Executive's introduction in September. I left on June 17, and visited Paris, Munich, Dusseldorf, Brussels, Copenhagen, Stockholm, Oslo, and London. With the exception of France, the news was good; product was selling well. Dvorak reports that some ex-employees he interviewed saw this tour as an ill-timed lark—a spree. The company wasn't stable and Osborne was off in Europe. If they only knew my feeling of helplessness at that time! With Salomon Brothers hinging their continued support on Jaunich's presence, the option of having the Board fire him disappeared. Yet I could do nothing while he was there.

I called Dennis Bovin from Copenhagen to see how preparations for the private placement were progressing. By this time Jaunich and I talked infrequently, and I was amazed to discover that he had still not given Salomon Brothers the go-ahead for the private placement. Had the May 25 Board meeting not expressly instructed him to move at once on this issue? According to Bovin, April year-end financial data, based on which the private placement would go ahead, was to be approved at the next Board meeting, scheduled for July 7.

I called Waite to find out what was going on. Jaunich apparently wanted audited numbers before any private placement commenced, Don explained, and the Board meeting had been postponed since the numbers would not be ready by July 7.

So I went on with my tour. In London I introduced Britain's Osborne dealers to the Executive. They were promised delivery of product in August.

It was late July before Bob Jaunich finally gave Salomon Brothers the go ahead to raise additional funds for Osborne Computer Corporation through a private placement of stock. By that time there was already negative press describing the company's misfortunes. It had begun in mid-June with an article by Paul Freiberger in *InfoWorld.* The rumors were too rampant to ignore.

Since I was out of town, Freiberger had called Jaunich to find out what substance, if any, there was to the rumors of Osborne's problems. According to Freiberger, Jaunich, who had no finesse with the press, was rude and abrupt; a very uncomplimentary article followed.

Bad news spreads with the speed of a flu virus. No sooner had I returned than Jaunich told me to get in touch with Eric Larson of *The Wall Street Journal.* Apparently, Jaunich had received word that Larson had picked up on the Freiberger story and was writing his own article. Interviewing a variety of vendors and dealers, Larson was getting perilously close to discovering the true depth of Osborne's problems. Had he published his findings in early July, his story would have dimmed the still-bright prospects for a private stock offering. It was imperative to draw Larson away from the facts, thereby giving Jaunich the needed time to complete a planned private stock placement.

I therefore carefully devised a story that would sell. It was plausible in that it spoke of a month without income. The Executive had been preannounced—so I said. The story made good copy by representing Adam Osborne as the brash hero-in-penitent pose. Eric Larson bought it and ran a story on the front page of *The Wall Street Journal* business section on Wednesday, July 13, 1983.

The Wall Street Journal story was not true. It was, in fact, the single and only time I have ever deliberately lied to the press. The facts are that the Executive was announced on April 17 and shipped during the first week of May—a miracle of punctuality by microcomputer industry standards. Subsequently the press reaffirmed with vigor my contention that in general they report on each other. That one story was rereported so frequently that most people today believe these are cross-verified facts coming from multiple sources: that Osborne Computer Corporation preannounced the Executive, and that this preannouncement contributed to the company's collapse.

As for rumors and gossip . . . both are always there. Ask any microcomputer manufacturer if they are working on new products and the manufacturer must answer either "Yes" or "No, we are planning to get out of the microcomputer business."

It is particularly noteworthy that industry pundits and seers bought the Executive preannouncement story as readily as the press did. Clearly some of the most prestigious consulting groups do not bother to check their facts before mouthing off.

With Eric Larson off the scent of the real story, the company returned to the matter of survival. As I had predicted, Executives were not selling at $2495 and Osborne I's were barely trickling out the door at $1995. Osborne I and Executive sales from May through August of 1983 are shown in Table 16.

The short-lived resurgence of June now gone, the canceled July 7 Board meeting was rescheduled for July 14 in an environment of growing gloom. Key points raised in this meeting included:

Table 16 **Total computer shipments between April and August, 1983.**

Month	*Executive*	*Osborne I*	*Osborne I Returns*	*Net Computers*
April	0	1469		1469
May	3857	1437		5295
June	5946	2480	859	7567
July	1637	667		2304
August	1282	1688		2970

1. Waite stated that there was approximately $17 million worth of Osborne I inventory on hand and another 15,000 Osborne I's could be built if $200,000 worth of parts were purchased.

2. Don Geyer was introduced to the Board, having just been hired as vice president and controller.
3. The slowdown in Executive sales was noted.
4. The Board agreed that the company's stock was now probably worth $1 per share. Based on this the terms of Jaunich's new employment contract with the company would change (as discussed fully later).
5. Jaunich told the Board that in addition to preparing for a possible private stock offering, the status of which he reviewed, he had also started working with the underwriters to find a large corporate investor. He presented the Board with a long list of potential investors that the underwriters had identified.

Shortly after the July 14 Board meeting, Jaunich did finally sign an employment contract. The terms of this final contract are shown in Table 17. Jaunich was paid a one-quarter-million-dollar bonus on July 21. He also received $121,153.83 in additional salary, via two checks dated July 21 and July 28.

Melchor seemed to be the only person trying to find more money for the company. He arranged for a London merchant banking firm to invest $10 million as part of the final $30-million refinancing that Waite had said the company needed. But Jaunich and Waite stated that representatives of Security Pacific Bank said they would seize the funds secured in London by Melchor to pay down the bank loan. The company was thus not prepared to accept the funds, since money was needed for day-to-day operation and product development. Certainly the London investors would not be prepared to see their money spent reducing bank debt.

Table 17 **A comparison of Jaunich's compensation on joining Osborne Computer Corporation, and after renegotiation.**

Compensation	*Original Agreement*	*Revised Contract*
Options to buy	100,000 shares	850,000 shares
Option price:	$16 per share	$1 per share
Vesting terms:	30% registered,	25% immediately
	of which 20% sold	25% July 15, 1984
	on public offering	25% July 15, 1985

Compensation	*Original Agreement*	*Revised Contract*
	Vesting terms for remainder not known but thought to be 35% each in Jan 1984 and 1985.	25% July 15, 1986 or 75% Dec 31, 1983 if paid for with promissory note.
Incentive options	None, but later awards likely.	100,000 shares
Option price:		$1 per share
Approximate % of outstanding shares fully diluted, after public offering, and probable $ value	2 8,000,000	9.5 38,000,000
Salary	$150,000 p.a.	$375,000 p.a. (retroactive to January)
Cash bonus	None	$500,000

So $10 million sat in an escrow account in New York, while Jaunich and Waite attempted to persuade Security Pacific Bank that the company should be allowed to survive. And while these discussions continued the climate for raising additional money deteriorated sharply. Right in the middle of the company's negotiations with Security Pacific Bank, Texas Instruments and Atari announced horrendous losses stemming from their microcomputer operations.

Finally, on the evening of Wednesday, August 3, Security Pacific Bank representatives relented. The company could indeed use the $10 million of London money for operations. But the very next morning, before the funds could be transferred from their escrow account in New York, Salomon Brothers called to announce that the private placement was off. Given the new, negative climate toward microcomputer investments resulting from the Texas Instruments and Atari debacles, Salomon Brothers did not feel they could raise $20 million for the company in a private placement. They noted also that the declining sales of Executives had done nothing to help the company's case.

One story reaching me at that time concerned Timex (themselves in trouble following a collapse in U.S. domestic sales of the Timex Sinclair ZX-81 home computer). In need of money Timex supposedly attempted a private placement, but just two analysts showed up for their presentation; and of these one left part way through the presentation. The bloom was off the rose.

The first real big personnel reduction occurred on August 2, when 202 people were terminated, most of them excellent workers who had given the company their best, none deserving what was happening to them at that time. Jim Ottinger and Bert Carson were terminated that day.

In a general meeting in the cafeteria, Jaunich and I talked to the survivors. It was a sad day for me and my sadness showed. Osborne Computer Corporation had been more than a plan to make money; it had been a dream. On August 2 the dream died. Many employees were in tears.

For Osborne Computer corporation the game was over. Faced with $30 million in accounts payable and monthly losses ranging between $1 and $2 million, the company was no longer an attractive buy. Who would spend $50 million or more on a product line that had never been technically spectacular? The distribution network and market position had propelled Osborne Computer Corporation to its heights. And by August of 1983 the distribution network was in disarray, while market position had been demolished under a barrage of negative publicity.

If questions arise about why Security Pacific Bank took such a hostile attitude towards the company, it should be noted that the bank's position, as reported in this book, is based on my recollections following discussions with Jaunich and Waite. At no time did I participate in any discussion with the bank. At the time this book was being written, I had never even met a representative from any one of the Company's three banks.

But assuming that Security Pacific Bank was indeed as intransigent as Jaunich and Waite reported, they probably destroyed Osborne's last chance for survival. Had they allowed the $10 million in British money to be used for company operations, the company may have to survived until the IBM compatible Executive was ready for market. And strong sales of that product could well have rescued the company.

Salomon Brothers, Smith Barney, and Rothschild Unterberg Towbin prepared a long list of potential acquirers for Osborne Computer Corporation. At the outset Salomon Brothers' Dennis Bovin said he thought there was a fifty-fifty chance of an acquirer being found. Jack Dulaney of Smith Barney said if an acquirer was found it would be a miracle. Nevertheless, through the month of August Osborne Computer Corporation frantically searched for an angel. A few companies showed interest until their financial people took a look at the numbers.

Every day there occurred a ritual exchange of telephone calls between Osborne Computer Corporation and Salomon Brothers. Every day the ranks of potential acquirers were further thinned.

At this late stage some vestiges of cooperation between Jaunich and myself appeared, but they rarely lasted for long. When I started talking directly to Dennis Bovin, Jaunich got angry.

"You are just pestering him," Jaunich snapped. "Who is he to believe represents the company?"

But by then I was no longer concerned with Jaunich's temper or feelings, and I persisted.

"Here," Jaunich snapped with ill humor as he threw the list of potential acquirers across the table at me. "You call. We can't both be doing it."

The week ending September 9 was the most nerve-wracking week of Osborne Computer Corporation's decline. There was no way out. In late August Security Pacific Bank had allowed the company to operate on the last of its Series B Preferred money, but every dime of receivables was being seized to pay off the company's bank loan. Management was reduced to clutching at any straw in the wind.

Close to the end, in late August, a delegation from NCR visited the company and left quite sure of their interest in acquiring Osborne Computer Corporation. But the visitors were engineers. When they took Osborne's financial numbers back to the home office, the deal quickly died.

A delegation from ITT visited the company during August and again on September 2. There was a positive note to these meetings, but the folks from ITT decided it would be best if they bought the company out of Chapter 11. Another meeting was scheduled for the week following the filing of bankruptcy. A delegation from Osborne Computer Corporation was to visit an ITT facility in Arizona to discuss Osborne's new products with some of ITT's technical staff.

Then on Friday September 9 word buzzed around the executive suite that the president of MATRA, France's huge defense conglomerate, had lost two nights of sleep over his excitement at the prospect of acquiring Osborne Computer Corporation. Jaunich scheduled a trip to the East Coast, but these last cold rays of sunshine could only illuminate an empty bank account and an absence of cash. No sale.

Finally it was clear that an acquirer would not be found. From then on it was simply a matter of days before the company ran out of money and had to file for bankruptcy.

A Board of Directors meeting was called on the evening of Friday, September 9 to authorize company management to file for bankruptcy the following week.

I tendered my resignation as a company employee the day before. I felt there was no point in my remaining in the company after Chapter 11 had been filed if Jaunich remained. With Jack Melchor I discussed forcing Jaunich to resign. Melchor dissuaded me. Given half an opportunity, Melchor pointed out, Jaunich would probably run laughing from the building.

During a bankruptcy the chief executive officer's primary task is to negotiate with banks and vendors. Having never dealt with either group during the company's declining months, I would have had to start from scratch handling both groups, which didn't seem like a good idea.

"No," Melchor advised. "Jaunich made this bed; let him sleep in it."

Perhaps of even greater consequence, I realized that once Chapter 11 had been filed—assuming I was no longer a company employee—I would be able to structure my own go-forward plan without having to deal with Jaunich or worry about conflicts of interest.

The final layoff was termed a furlough, since no severance or vacation pay was available. It occurred on September 9. That day 312 people left, leaving roughly 80 people behind.

With the smell of doom and gloom in their nostrils, the press swooped down on the building and the telephones started to ring off the hook. Executives wandered back and forth in those surrealistic twilight hours, exchanging expressions of hope while the press stationed themselves at the door to extract statements from anyone they could get to talk. But unlike the dark meeting of August 2 in the company cafeteria, on September 9 I spent an hour or two at the Pot Belli Deli with terminated employees. I bought no drinks for myself that day; employees bought all my drinks for me. The terminated employees were with me, and I with them.

A QUESTION OF RESERVES

Complete financial data are given in Appendix B for the fiscal years ending November 1982, February and May 1983, and for the quarters ending February and May 1983. Table 18 compares year-end and quarter-end consolidated statements of earnings. One fact becomes immediately clear. Up to the end of February 1983 Osborne Computer Corporation's operating loss was quite small. In fact there was an operating profit, strictly speaking, since the year-ending-February numbers include almost $3.5 million of reserves. The large losses later added to the fiscal year ending February 1983 resulted entirely from the creation of new reserves.

Reserves (for readers who do not understand such things) are an accounting technique which financial people use to make losses from management sins show up in the same time period that the sins were committed.

For example, suppose a candlemaker makes new, deluxe candles for $10 each and sells them to candle stores for $20 each. Then the bottom suddenly falls out of the deluxe candle market, and stores are only prepared to pay $7.50 each for these new, deluxe candles. Suppose the unfortunate candlemaker already has 10,000 candles in his warehouse when the market collapses. An auditor would not allow the candlemaker to take a $2.50 loss on each candle when he can sell them in the future for $7.50 each. Instead the auditor would tell the candlemaker that he had to set up a "reserve account" for $25,000. This reserve account would become a current $25,000 expense item. When the candlemaker sells off his candles for $7.50 each, the reserve account is reduced by $2.50 for every candle sold.

If all goes well, the candlemaker will sell off his 10,000 candles for $7.50 apiece, the reserve account will be reduced to zero, and the loss will have been properly recorded in the prior time period when the candlemaker was stupid enough to build the 10,000 overpriced candles.

Now suppose the deluxe candle market worsens. The candlemaker successfully sells 5000 candles for $7.50 each, but he only gets $5 each for the remaining 5000 candles. The $12,500 extra loss must show up in a future time period, and the auditor will have to hang his head in shame for not creating an adequate reserve.

On the other hand, suppose the deluxe candle market picks up. If, after selling 1000 candles for $7.50 each, the candlemaker gets his full $20 each for the remaining 9000 candles, then he will be able to report a profit of $12.50 on each candle sold at the higher price and $22,500 of the loss he took previously will now show up as extra profit. Thus, the previous time period will inaccurately look less profitable than it should have, and the future time period will inaccurately look more profitable by the same amount.

The question of whether Osborne Computer Corporation's finances

Table 18 **Quarterly and annual financial results compared.**

Thousands of dollars, for fiscal year ending:	Nov 27 1982	Feb 26 1983(B)	Feb 26 1983(C)	May 28 1983(D)	May 28 1983(E)
Net sales:	68783	92789	92789	104759	104759
Cost and expenses:					
Cost of sales:	50795	71829	70668	68481	88181
Reserve for product discontinuation:					
R & D	1643	3618	3618	5917	5917
Marketing	12745	19982	19848	27940	27940
G & A	3531	5088	5088	7585	7585
Total costs and expenses:	68714	100517	103517	110123	129623
Operating income:	69	(7728)	(10728)	(5164)	(24864)
Interest and other expenses:	1090	1355	1355	1590	1590
Net loss:	(1021)	(9083)	(12083)	(6754)	(26454)

Thousands of dollars, for fiscal quarter ending:	Feb 26 1983(A)	May 28 1983(A)
Net sales:	34377	21985
Costs and expenses:		
Cost of sales:	23797	17395
Reserve for product discontinuation:		3500
R & D	1700	2225
Marketing	7475	9565
G & A	1530	2835
Total cost and expenses:	34502	35520
Operating income:	(125)	(13535)
Interest and other expenses:	520	1175
Net loss:	(645)	(14710)

(A) These are unaudited quarterly results from internal reports.

(B) was the first, and (C) the final result for the fiscal year restated to end in February of 1983. Neither use the quarterly results shown above.

(D) This is the result for the fiscal year ending May of 1983, without the reserves. (E) is the same results with reserves included.

Table 19 **A summary of all reserve accounts created and the months to which they were assigned.**

Reserve	*Jan*	*Feb*	*May*	*Sept*
A/R disputes		0	100000	187551
Bad debt international	0	40000	40000	
Sales returns		614000	558400	169422
Al'ce bad debt	410696	330492	575000	936372
OCC 1 NRV		0	0	8653111
Other inventory	1086043	5666465	7576333	800122
Price protect		0	1000000	0
Warranty	80000	0	0	(37653)
Payroll		2800	342979	23491
Vacation	243961	273452	356321	246965
Sick leave	14108	16612	21787	37488
Bonuses	136759	0	25000	25000
Advertising	317146	392848	65206	270638
Sales tax	3839	(65)	1447	8097
Interest		17590	45030	210571
Legal		0	200000	180841
Audit		238750	221250	221250
Warranty card		667863	1880403	1821706
Prompt pay			200000	200000
Commission Pay		18000	1500	0
Warranty repair		250000	141125	95872
dBASEII promotion		0	150631	126091
P-system		0	411264	409018
Personal Pearl		0	169944	84355
Co-op advertising		0	697662	857626
Unaudit liability	2108155	3904649	4862015	2071077
Misc. (software)	3595551	4002105	3597093	3440741
Total debit:	0	61669233	17814206	0
Total credit:	0	70050536	25273054	0
Total balance:	7996258	16395561	23240389	21079750

Table 20 **Reserve accounts established and equivalent entries on various financial statements.**

Reserve	*Balance Sheet Equivalent*
A/R disputes	
Bad debt international	
Sales returns	
Al'ce bad debt	
OCC 1 NRV	OCC 1 NRV
Other inventory	OCC 1 NRV & contracts & terminations of facilities
Price protect	OCC 1 related end of life provision
Warranty	Promotions: dBASEII, Personal Pearl, unit giveaways, extended warranty
Payroll	
Vacation	
Sick leave	
Bonuses	
Advertising	
Sales tax	
Interest	
Legal	Legal/audit
Audit	Legal/audit
Warranty card	
Prompt pay	
Comission pay	
Warranty repair	
dBASEII promo	Promotions: dBASEII, Personal Pearl, unit giveaways, extended warranty
P-system	
Personal Pearl	Promotions: dBASEII, Personal Pearl, unit giveaways, extended warranty
Co-op advertising	
Unaudit Liability	Promotions: dBASEII, Personal Pearl, unit giveaways, extended warranty, legal/audit, and other
Misc.(software)	Software: Softech, Peachtree, miscellaneous & Vixen 5″ Prototype

were really out of control, as Jaunich charged and the press reported, must be judged by looking at actual operating results together with the reserve accounts that were created.

Unfortunately, reserve accounts represent the last bastion of pure speculation in the otherwise sterile and precise world of accounting. Nowhere is there more fertile ground for manipulating numbers and creating distortions than in reserve accounting—in particular when someone wants to paint a picture that is unnecessarily bleak. After all, what auditor is going to tell a client that he is being excessively conservative?

Table 19 summarizes $19.7 million of reserve accounts that ultimately went into the year-end statement for a fiscal year ending May 1983. An additional $3.34 million of reserves were assigned to earlier time periods, for a total of $23.04 million of reserves on the books as of May 1983. Table 19 also shows the subsequent depletion of reserves. Of the $23.2 million May end reserves, just $2.1 million had been consumed when the company filed for bankruptcy in September. The bulk of this $2.1 million was consumed in a single "unaudited liabilities" account that represents spending committed in an earlier time period, but not recorded by accounting as having been spent until later. This is the only reserve account in Table 19 that truly represents inadequate accounting controls. (Table 20 will only be of value to a student who needs to establish a correlation between Table 19 and the original company data.)

A QUESTION OF INVENTORY

Two curious, unreported conditions at Osborne Computer Corporation under Jaunich need to be addressed before any conclusions can be drawn as to what really went wrong: Osborne I inventory and the reserve accounting surrounding this inventory.

The question of Osborne I inventory will be examined first.

In early February, Jaunich said he favored ordering inventory to build another 20,000 Osborne I's. At that time the company still had sufficient inventory on order to build Osborne I's for shipment through the end of April, given forecast sales levels.

"What if the Executive slips another three months?" Jaunich asked.

I was horrified by the prospect of buying any more Osborne I inventory. "You've got to be out of your mind," I replied. "Following the Executive announcement in mid-April, Osborne I sales will die anyway. And the Executive can't slip much, fifty units are in Beta test." ("Beta test'' means units were in the hands of friendly users who were checking them out.)

A three-month slip in schedule seemed highly unlikely. And even if there was a slip, it would be better to sell nothing rather than try to sell something for which there was no longer a market.

''By mid-March the Osborne I backlog will be gone,'' I warned, ''and you had better be out hustling for sales again.''

Taking up the same theme, Jim Ottinger met with Georgette Psaris (then still vice president for domestic marketing) and Ron Brown (vice president for international operations) and suggested that the company plan on building an extra 15,000 Osborne I's.

''We agreed to take another 6000 Osborne I's,'' Georgette noted in her customary, methodical manner. ''Fifteen hundred would be exported, and I would sell the remainder domestically.''

But I would have none of it. The plan had always been to stop building Osborne I's in advance of the Executive and to dry out the pipeline before introducing the new product. The company had done this in advance of the injection-molded–blue-case Osborne I's a year earlier. For the Executive, similar plans had been formulated in an Executive Committee meeting of September 22, 1982, and had been subsequently referred to in Executive Committee and Board meetings dated October 27, November 1, December 1, and December 8.

My alarm grew again when Ottinger told me that Jaunich had already authorized purchase orders for 19,000 additional Osborne I's.

''He's out of his mind,'' Ottinger said, a hesitant laugh tinging his voice. ''I cut the order back to 14,000 extra units without telling Bob.''

I then went to Jack Melchor, who agreed that no extra Osborne I inventory whatsoever should be purchased.

At the Board meeting of February 28, Osborne I inventory was discussed at great length. Melchor, Rubinstein, Hogan, and I all recollect leaving from that meeting with assurances from Jaunich that he would only buy a small quantity of Osborne I inventory—enough to complete partial kits, thereby using up components that might otherwise be scrapped. The minutes of that Board meeting read as follows:

> Turning to the Company's profitability, Mr. Jaunich pointed out that pricing was the key to the Company's future. He noted that the Company would price aggressively high with future introduction of products and that the price could always be reduced in the event that competition eroded the Company's market share and/or sales. Mr.

> Jaunich pointed out that the important thing was that the Company not lose control of its growth and if it had to give up a certain amount of sales in order to keep control of that growth, it would do so. Mr. Jaunich noted that he had not yet been able to examine the inventory exposure for the OCC-1. The board discussed at length the topic that the Company should avoid all write offs on the OCC-1. Mr. Jaunich and Mr. Ottinger reported that based on current plans and information the company's exposure was approximately $3–4 million for the OCC-1.

And elsewhere in the same Board meeting's minutes:

> He (Mr. Ottinger) observed that the company intended to reserve against inventory to reflect potential write-offs for the OCC-1 once the Osborne Executive was introduced and sales for the Osborne I diminished.

Following the company's bankruptcy Jaunich publicly denied on more than one occasion that any extra Osborne I inventory had been ordered in February or March of 1983. The facts contradict Jaunich's assertion.

Table 21 summarizes the total of Osborne I inventory orders placed between January and April of 1983. Complete purchase order details are given in Appendix A. Figure 2 shows the curious timing of these purchase orders, taking into account the Osborne I sales levels recorded at the time the purchase orders were placed.

Table 21 also shows inventory that could have been used to build either Osborne I's or Executives, since these inventory items provided an additional opportunity, not taken, to use up existing Osborne I inventory by diverting it to the Executive production line.

Despite extensive research there is still significant confusion surrounding Osborne I purchases. It is not clear when the inventory order between February and April was delivered. A significant amount had not been delivered at the end of April, which is not surprising, given how recent some of the purchase orders were. But documents researched show that most of the inventory appears to have been delivered by June, as shown in Table 21. A good deal of the inventory covered by January purchase orders also appears to have been delivered between March and June. If Jaunich had lived up to the commitment that he made to the Board at the end of February, no new purchase orders should have been issued for Osborne I inventory, existing purchase orders should have been canceled wherever possible, and common inventory already in-house should have been diverted to the Executive.

How many dollars does this amount to? Table 21 shows roughly $5.8 million worth of purchase orders placed in February, March and April. However, at the Board meeting of April 29, Waite stated that the company had 15,000 Osborne I's in parts and finished goods. At the Board meeting of July 14, the number had not changed. Mr. Waite stated that with the purchase of $200,000 worth of inventory, an additional 15,000 Osborne I's could be built.

In mid-February the company was production-bound on Osborne I's, with less than a week's worth of inventory on many key parts. There was probably usuable inventory equivalent to less than 1000 Osborne I's. Also, at the end of January there was, in-house, a certain amount of scrap inventory that Ottinger estimated to be worth $3 million. This data can be used in conjunction with sales and major returns figures for the months of February through June to compute the Osborne I inventory received, as shown in Table 22.

In February the Company had planned on building approximately 15,000 Osborne I's to meet March and April sales projections. Therefore, of the 40,000 Osborne I's worth of inventory shown in Table 22 purchased between February and the end of June, roughly 25,000 units' worth are, theoretically, excess purchases that could have and should have been avoided. However, this number includes roughly $3 million worth of unusable inventory which, as noted above, Jim Ottinger reported at the February Board meeting had to be scrapped.

Inventory for 25,000 Osborne I's is equivalent to approximately $14 million. This number is computed by adding the ending inventory and the inventory in shipped goods, then subtracting from this total the beginning inventory. Since the beginning inventory included scrap, this must be accounted for. Subtracting the $3 million of scrap reported by Jim Ottinger at the February Board meeting, leaves $11 million worth of inventory that was purchased unnecessarily since the end of February 1983.

By closing the warehouse doors to all excess Osborne I inventory at the end of February, as Jaunich had assured the Board he would do, some $11 million worth of unnecessary Osborne I inventory expenditures could have been avoided.

Table 21 **Parts ordered between January and June of 1983 showing number of Osborne I's that could be built with the quantity of parts ordered, and parts not received at end of June.**

	Jan	*Feb*	*March*	*April to June*	*Remaining to be shipped in June*
Plastics					
Front bezel	12776	2200	29776	933	16
Keyboard bezel	9704	2000	53972	0	0
Handle pocket	11120	0	26862	0	0
Case top	28912	0	37217	0	0
Vent cover	11080	0	50384	0	0
Cord pocket	10208	0	49476	0	0
Cord cover	8665	0	51066	0	0
Knob fabrication	30030	0	0	0	0
Knob assembly	0	0	35550	0	0
Case bottom	9218	0	22351	0	0
Chassis assembly	12260	0	25248	0	0
Keyboard case	27932	0	2009	0	0
Keyboards					
Keyboards	0	1600	21106	27	0
Keyswitch arrays	0	0	12761	28838	0
Electronics					
CPU boards	28200	22	0	0	0
CPU board revs	92600	702	0	0	0
Disk electronics	30500	170	5000	0	0
5″ Monitors	0	10980	0	0	0
Power supplies	0	0	10000	0	0
Disk drives	40	11594.5	2250	0	0
Total $ value of orders:					
For OI only	8345219	2296837	1294369	8572	0
For OI or Exec	845130	47073	1497065	227400	0

Table 22 **A summary of Osborne I sales and inventory purchases between February and July of 1983.**

Month	*Units in Starting Inventory*	*Units Sold*	*Special Returns Units*	*End Inventory-Computed Units*	*End Inventory-Reported Units*	*Number of Units That Could Be Built with Inventory Bought*
February	1000	11785				
March		9914				
April		1469			15000	37168
May	15000	1437		13563		
June	13563	2480	859	11942	15000	40226

Chapter Nine SOME EXPLANATIONS

There are three ways to explain Bob Jaunich's involvement as chief executive officer in the collapse of Osborne Computer Corporation. First, an argument may be made that he tried to manipulate the company's fortunes in an effort to improve his personal position. Second, it could be argued that he was thrust into the throes of a runaway environment that was beyond rescue. Or third, he simply wasn't competent.

Only circumstantial supposition supports the first argument, and its presentation in this chapter should be read strictly as the authors' supposition and opinion. Moreover, even the facts upon which arguments in this chapter are based might be flawed. The authors of this book employed a research assistant who, for four months, collected and analyzed data; however, records at Osborne Computer Corporation were already in some disarray at the time we were collecting data. I was no longer an officer of the Corporation during critical time periods in 1983, so my files did not contain much information. Although we have not knowingly included any erroneous data, and we are unaware of any possible data that might cast significant new light on the decline of Osborne Computer Corporation, readers should nevertheless keep in mind these caveats before reaching their own conclusions. I would note, however, that Jack Melchor, Les Hogan and Seymour Rubinstein have all read Chapter 6, 7, 8, and 9 of this book, and although I neither asked for nor received an endorsement of the contents from any of these three, none suggested any changes to the text.

A simple motive, greed, supports the first argument. Table 17 shows that Jaunich's percentage ownership of Osborne Computer Corporation stock, on a fully diluted basis after all options had been exercised and new stock had been issued, would have increased from 2 percent of the outstanding shares to 9.5 percent. Moreover, the 2 percent would have decreased to 1.6 percent, since Jaunich was due to sell 20,000 shares of his stock at a March public offering. In contrast, his position after renegotiating his contract with the Board in July would have left him in effective control of the company—by far the largest single stockholder, and well positioned to further increase his holdings via future stock options.

Assuming that he could have brought the company back to its overall value, as estimated by underwriters in February of 1983, Jaunich's personal financial position would have improved from approximately $8 million in February 1983 (100,000 shares valued at approximately $80 per share) to $38 million, (950,000 shares at $40 a share). Nothing to sneeze at, particularly for someone who, like Jaunich, measured a man by the fortune he amassed.

While the incentive is certainly there, conclusive evidence is lacking. Therefore the same circumstances will be used first to support the argument that Jaunich manipulated Osborne Computer Corporation's finances to his personal advantage, then to argue that Jaunich was an honorable man doing his desperate best to cope with an unmanageable mess.

Both Dvorak and I dismiss the argument that Jaunich was simply incompetent. His career prior to joining Osborne Computer Corporation eloquently attests to the man's competence. I think that Jaunich is one of the most intelligent, capable, and competent men I have ever met. Assuming that Jaunich was trying to improve his position, he first had to force a postponement of the public offering. Following a public offering, he would have had little opportunity to improve his personal position within the company, under the glare of public scrutiny. By plunging the company into one more artificially created, temporary financial crisis for which he could blame prior management (just as every elected government blames its predecessor), he could position himself as the "white knight" who turned the company around. The contract he renegotiated for himself in the depths of the crisis would appear to be legitimate compensation for a corporate savior.

I speculate that Jaunich could easily have caused the first postponement by providing cautious, hesitant, or uncertain responses when in January the underwriters were performing their due diligence interviews—for example: "I have been here too short a time to comment on the strengths of existing management,'' or ''It is impossible to say that the new products will be introduced on time or will be well received.''

There is no evidence that Jaunich did indeed make comments such as these, however. Although such comments may not have affected lesser souls, there is no doubt they would have given Salomon Brothers reason for pause.

Following the January postponement of a public offering, it would have been easy to manipulate the apparent financial condition of Osborne Computer Corporation, or any similar thinly capitalized, high-growth company. Keeping such a company under financial control is like walking a tightrope anyway.

To understand this point, consider again the poor candlemaker who finished up with large reserve accounts after making too many expensive candles. Prior to his problems let's suppose his business had been increasing at a fast clip. He did $20,000 worth of business in month 1, thereafter increasing his business at the rate of $10,000 per month. Thus he would have to use $10,000 of revenues from month 1 sales, received (if he was very lucky) in month 2, to buy inventory for $30,000 worth of business in month 3. Impossible! The candlemaker would need a bank loan, easy enough to obtain, since we presume he made a profit each month, on paper if not in cash. Together with his accounts receivable and his inventory, that would certainly be enough to get him his bank loan.

Suddenly the candlemaker is faced with a $25,000 reserve. He tells his banker, Oh, no!

As far as the banker is concerned, the candlemaker's loan collateral has just declined by $25,000. But worse! The candlemaker's inventory may be of questionable value, so his collateral may have decreased much more than the $25,000 amount of the reserve. The candlemaker's ability to borrow is destroyed. He is in deep trouble.

If Jaunich did indeed manipulate the company's fortunes, then what he did was, in my opinion, exquisite in its simple brilliance. He bought excess Osborne I inventory while encouraging through inactivity a decline in Osborne I sales. That is equivalent to a president hired by the candlemaker buying candle wax for the expensive candles, after it has become obvious that the expensive candles are not selling. Instead of being an asset to back loans, the candle wax and finished candles end up in reserve accounts, turning assets into liabilities and profits into losses.

Based on the facts presented, it is my opinion that in February Jaunich started buying excess Osborne I inventory. I believe this had to be done carefully since the company had long planned on removing Osborne I's from the dealers' shelves in advance of the Executive introduction. It was therefore necessary to break up purchase orders and scatter them across a lot of time with as much confusion and ambiguity as possible, in particular because much of the inventory was being purchased after it had become obvious that Osborne I sales were taking a nosedive. Thus I note that fifty-six separate purchase orders averaging $49,800 each were issued in March, compared to thirty-three purchase orders averaging $278,500 each in January and eighteen February invoices averaging $130,200 each. I would suggest that an advantage of issuing small purchase orders was that relatively low-level personnel could sign them. Only one purchase order was found bearing Jaunich's signature—scratched out.

Recent conversations with Ottinger and Carr disclosed that during March Jaunich continued to authorize purchase of Osborne I inventory based on sales projections stretching into June and even July. This was in direct conflict with assurances Jaunich gave at the February Board meeting. Psaris has not been able to shed much light on these events, since at the time Jaunich had not only stopped inviting her to attend product planning meetings, but was not even informing her of scheduled meetings.

Fig. 2 illustrates the timing of inventory purchases against the backdrop of evaporating sales. From an average of 500–600 Osborne I sales per day, by late March sales had collapsed to roughly 200 per day, and the relative decline in domestic sales was even worse. Moreover, because a softening in orders precedes any sales decline by a couple of weeks, by early March Jaunich should have known that real problems were brewing. Yet the inventory kept pouring in. In my opinion, the easy part was to encourage the decline in Osborne I sales. Jaunich needed no help in doing this. New product rumors were rampant. And coming off a boom selling season, Osborne Computer Corporation badly needed a dramatic program to keep Osborne I sales flowing in the weeks preceding the Executive introduction. For five months (effectively) the dBASEII special offer had been in effect. In fact, the dBASEII offer officially terminated at the end of January. However, all orders received before the end of the month were included in the special offer and it is my recollection that these orders accounted for much of the February sales volume. However, I have not been able to obtain documentation to support this recollection. Any special offer in effect for such a long time becomes a new de facto standard price. Ending the special offer with nothing to replace it was equivalent to raising the price of the Osborne I. I was in favor of a price cut to $1495, and in the absence of that some spectacular increase in value. Psaris wanted to bundle a free modem with every Osborne I. But endless committee meetings dragging into mid-April prevented the implementation of any new program that might have stemmed the rapidly deteriorating sales figures.

In my opinion the program introduced in April was anemic. A data base program called "Personal Pearl" was to be given away with every Osborne I until June 1. Also, dealers would receive two free service warranties with each new Osborne I ordered.

Personal Pearl had been given away free with modems earlier in the year with little success. Modems allow computers to communicate over telephone lines. They cost less than $300. I felt there was no basis for assuming that Personal Pearl would be any more effective at moving the much higher priced Osborne I.

Giving the dealer two service policies with each new Osborne I ordered would supposedly encourage sales, since the dealer had roughly $500 in value that he could use as he saw fit: either to increase his profit or to pass on to customers in the form of lower prices. I think the flaw in this plan was fundamental: dealers never have and never will sell a product for the manufacturer. It is the manufacturer's job to bring customers into the dealer's showroom. Dealers were already overstocked with Osborne I's. To take advantage of the free service warranty program, first they had to sell their oversupply of Osborne I's, plus an increment of additional Osborne I's—all to a reluctant customer base. To sell all of them dealers would have to run ads whose message was: "Hey! I have this thing you don't think you need, but let me tell you why you should buy it." This is the very thing that no retailer will ever do.

And so the stage was set for the inventory purchased in February and March to collide with the sales decline being encouraged through inactivity and anticipation of a new product.

To ensure that no one would question the motives behind these actions, I personally believe that Jaunich presented himself as working toward a public offering. In the course of this he did two things during April that, in retrospect, I find very curious.

First, he sent all stockholders his letter, dated April 6, the text of which is reprinted in Chapter 7. The odd timing of this letter is illus-

Figure 2 **Osborne 1 average daily shipments**

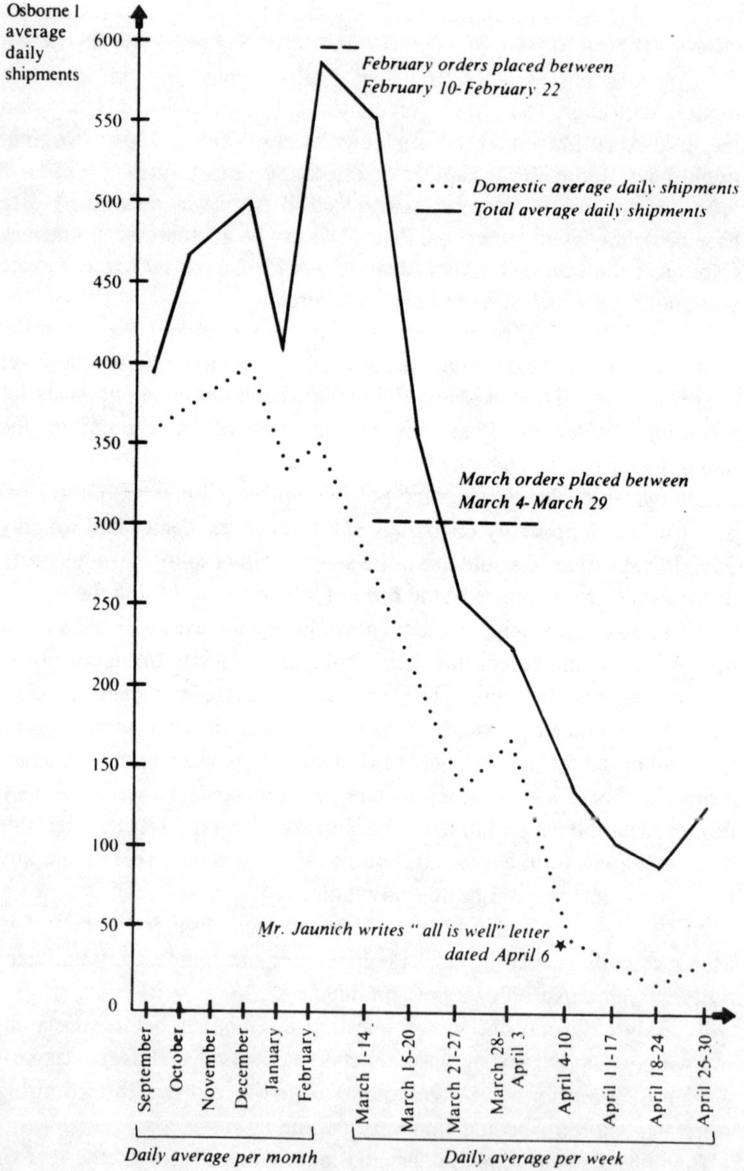

trated in Figure 2. This letter makes no mention of either the collapse in Osborne I sales or of Jaunich's fears that the Executive introduction might be delayed further—a fear, I believe, he must have had to justify continuing to issue purchase orders for Osborne I inventory through the end of March and into April.

If Jaunich genuinely thought that Executive shipments might well be delayed by two or three months, I suggest that it should have been included in his letter of April 6, and the investors providing the company with letters of credit (myself included) should have been warned of his fear.

If, on the other hand, Jaunich did not believe there would be a significant delay in the Executive introduction—which is why he made no mention of the fact to stockholders or potential letter-of-credit investors—then in my opinion he should have closed the warehouse doors to incoming Osborne I inventory, canceling every conceivable Osborne I purchase order, diverting common components to the Executive, and selling off surplus inventory wherever possible. After all, by early April the slowdown in Osborne I shipments was blatantly evident.

The second curious event, in my opinion, was the meeting with the underwriters at the Hyatt-Grand Central on the morning of Friday, April 22. I personally recall at that meeting that Jaunich said the company would probably lose $4 million for the fiscal year ending February with the quarter ending May likely to be breakeven. But it is my personal opinion that Jaunich had to know what he was saying was highly improbable. Some $6 million worth of additional Osborne I inventory was pouring into the company, and he had made no attempt to reduce spending in the face of a sharp revenue decline. With no Executive sales and few Osborne I's being shipped in April, it should have been clear to Jaunich that the quarter ending May had to be a financial disaster. In my opinion it should also have been obvious to anyone who understood reserves that, on looking at current sales levels, Waite was going to increase reserves across the board, thereby skewering the fiscal year ending February as well as the quarter ending May.

In my opinion, Jaunich's actions during April prevented anyone from becoming suspicious or nervous. I recall his end-of-month revelations startling everyone. If Jaunich had planned the whole thing, no move was so clever as lulling everyone into believing that things were going well, then suddenly presenting a disaster.

It is intriguing to note that, as shown in Table 23, between 1971 and

1974 while Jaunich was at Memorex, large reserve accounts were created and subsequently brought in as profits.

Beginning with the Board meeting of April 29, my course of action was determined largely by two individuals: Les Hogan and Dennis Bovin of Salomon Brothers.

Les Hogan consistently maintained that Jaunich was manipulating the company. Throughout March, April, and May he was in favor of throwing Jaunich out. There were occasions when Jack Melchor was tempted to agree with Hogan.

On the other hand Dennis Bovin emphasized at every meeting that Salomon Brothers' participation in any rescue effort for the company depended on Jaunich's presence. It would have appeared, in fact, that Salomon Brothers was taking Jaunich and his management team public rather than Osborne Computer Corporation.

Table 23 **Memorex Financial Information.**

Memorex Five-Year Summary
Years end December 31
(thousands except per-share amounts)

	1975	1974	1973	1972	1971
Summary of Operations*					
Revenues:					
Sales	$162,139	$118,297	$ 83,991	$ 83,991	$ 64,554
Rental & service	101,855	99,330	92,932	78,322	45,647
Total revenues	263,994	217,627	176,923	145,422	110,201
Costs and expenses:					
Cost of sales, rental & service	163,651	147,743	138,392	86,146	74,553
Other costs & expenses	67,245	60,181	103,427	45,247	45,247
Interest expense	15,268	18,675	20,487	19,951	16,271
Total expenses	246,164	226,599	262,306	151,344	143,753
Income before taxes and extraordinary credits	17,830	(8,972)	(85,383)	(5,922)	(33,552)

	1975	1974	1973	1972	1971
Provision (credit) for income taxes	9,585	—	4,925	752	(5,837)
Income (loss) before extraordinary credits	8,245	(8,972)	(90,308)	(6,674)	(27,715)

	Primary	Fully Diluted	Primary			
Net income (loss) per common share:						
Before extraordinary credit	$1.74	$1.72	$(2.08)	$(20.96)	$(1.60)	$(7.10)
Net income (loss)	3.80	3.77	(2.08)	(20.96)	(1.66)	(7.10)
Proforma net income (loss) per common share:						
Before extraordinary credit	$1.03	$1.01	$(2.60)	—	—	—
Net income (loss)	3.09	3.06	(2.60)	—	—	—
Common shares & equivalents	4,740	4,781	4,314	4,309	4,029	3,901

	1975	1974	1973	1972	1971
Operating Data*					
Total Revenue:					
Equipment	$156,307	$116,043	$ 92,678	$ 71,993	$ 41,998
Media	107,687	101,584	84,245	73,429	68,203
Income (loss) before interest, provision for income taxes & extraordinary credits:					
Equipment	27,942	(1,267)	(71,380)	—	—
Media	5,156	10,970	6,484	—	—

	1975	1974	1973	1972	1971
International revenue	112,000	87,000	75,000	59,000	41,000
R & D expenses	9,282	7,462	3,658	11,159	14,132
Depreciation & amortization	40,532	46,323	59,162	33,560	26,618
Financial Position at Year-end*					
Cash & temporary investments	$ 40,182	$ 11,783	$ 4,099	$ 8,828	$ 8,649
Inventories	44,797	50,747	58,779	44,710	46,754
Equip. for lease, net	61,067	84,878	92,654	111,923	93,142
Notes payable	117,562	163,117	226,022	182,626	198,198
Convertible subordinated debentures	68,045	75,000	75,000	75,000	75,000
Shareholders' equity (deficiency)	3,091	(23,677)	(86,857)	3,437	5,041

* Restated for the effect of research and development costs retroactively charged to operations as incurred:

	1973	1972	1971
Net income (loss):			
Previously reported	$(119,090)	$ 1,193	$(13,390)
Currently reported	(90,308)	(6,674)	(27,715)
Restatement amount credit (charge)	$ 28,782	$ (7,867)	$(14,325)
Per share	6.67	(1.96)	(3.67)

I was as panicked as everyone else. I felt that it was no time for vendettas or acrimony. By early May I knew that I had no choice but to act as a calming influence. Pragmatically there was little alternative. Until late July the overwhelming probability was that a rescue would be successful; therefore creating dissension made no sense whatsoever. So I kept the press away from Jaunich and the company's problems, and I attempted to smooth the friction between Jaunich and the Board, which constantly simmered just below the surface.

In my opinion, Jaunich's apparent determination not to liquidate excess inventory (which was my perception) and his lack of enthusiasm for fund-raising efforts following the April crisis were also unusual.

Faced with a cash crisis and huge inventory reserve accounts, I believe it was critical that Osborne I finished goods and inventory be unloaded quickly and for any price above the established reserve. In my opinion it is fundamental that one liquidate large reserve accounts by any means possible, grabbing every dollar above the reserve that can be found. In my opinion the most galling Jaunich inaction, cited by Fred Brown and myself, was his continual failure to agree that Osborne I's should be dumped. Recall that at the end of April Brown negotiated the sale of 4000–6000 Osborne I's to Bob Leviton at a price well above the reserve and in fact only a few dollars below the company's normal net revenue. Brown's negotiations with TWA offered Osborne the chance to sell off most of the remaining Osborne I inventory. Nothing came of the plans. Brown blamed Jaunich's office for failing to make a decision. In my opinion, the sales should have been made, and quickly, circumventing price-protection issues by whatever creative strategy the situation demanded.

Regarding fundraising, I recall that everyone at the April 29 Board meeting—the underwriters included—stressed the need to get new money into the company as quickly as possible by approaching every available source. At the time Melchor was the only person trying to raise money for the company. I recall his efforts annoyed Jaunich, who on more than one occasion complained to me that Melchor's money-raising efforts were antagonizing Dennis Bovin and should therefore be stopped.

I recall that Jaunich claimed the fundraising delay was necessary, since an audited and stable financial statement for the year ending May had to be ready before anyone raised money for the company. Osborne Computer Corporation had sought no such delay a year earlier when bringing in $10 million to get out of the 1982 crisis; nor had an audited statement preceded any effort by Melchor to raise money, including the sale of Series B Preferred shares at the end of May. In my opinion, full disclosure would have allowed any sophisticated group of investors to perform adequate due diligence, even in early May when the microcomputer market was still red hot.

And yet it was late July, two and a half months later, before Jaunich gave Salomon Brothers the go-ahead to proceed with a private placement—after he had renegotiated his new contract with Osborne's Board. And, in my opinion these negotiations may account for Jaunich's fundraising inactivity. I believe that his negotiation stance would have been severely weakened had Osborne Computer Corporation quickly sold off its excess inventory, escaped its cash bind, and brought in new equity. I believe this turnaround had to wait until Jaunich had taken care of himself, negotiating a new employment contract that met his objectives.

On May 25 the first of many new contracts were agreed upon by the Board and Jaunich, and then only because Melchor refused to release the Series B Preferred funds without such an agreement. The terms of this first agreement were similar to that shown in Table 17; however, in my opinion Osborne Computer Corporation's stock price was not yet low enough, so "junior stock" (a stock option tax dodge) was used. Jaunich's bonus was to have an outside guarantor but not to be paid until the Series C financing had been completed.

Between the end of April and May 25, Jaunich frequently told me that he had done nothing about his own compensation, being too busy with the company's crisis. But I was in continuous contact with Melchor, who had a very different story to tell. According to Melchor negotiations with Jaunich had begun almost immediately; however, each time an agreement appeared to be at hand Jaunich would introduce a new set of demands. This unending negotiation came out into the open at the tense May 25 Board meeting. Nerves were so frayed that when Melchor raised his hand to scratch his nose, Jaunich's hot temper flared one more time. He snapped that there was no point continuing with an explanation of his demands if Melchor was going to interrupt him all the time. But still no final agreement was signed until late July.

That final agreement allowed Jaunich to pay himself more than $360,000 in advance of the Series C financing. He paid himself the money promptly, roughly six weeks before the company filed bankruptcy.

By mid-July everything was in place for a spectacular turnaround—everything, that is, except fate. In late July the devastating announcements about Texas Instruments' and Atari's huge losses put the lid on any money flowing into the microcomputer hardware business. But for this twist of fate, there is little doubt in my mind that even in late July the underwriters could have raised $20 million privately to augment the $10 million already raised by Melchor and sitting in an escrow account in New York. With these funds I believe that the company could have floated with ease into the Christmas selling season, at which time the existing Osborne I inventory would probably have sold out quickly. Executive sales would have revived, and the Executive PC, which was due to be introduced in November, would have added new glamour, along with the Vixen, which would have been introduced early in 1984.

In a strong selling environment, I believe the bulk of the reserve accounts would probably have been unnecessary and would have shown up in 1984 profits. The company would probably have gone public in the first quarter of 1984.

In my opinion, no one would have argued. The private placement investors would have tripled their money in less than a year. The venture capital community would all have made a profit, and since I was planning on leaving anyway, I would have kept my suspicion to myself, along with $8 million worth of stock.

But the private placement never did occur. Within five weeks of Salomon Brothers abandoning the private placement, the company filed for protection under Chapter 11 of the bankruptcy code, with its reported assets just $5 million less than its reported liabilities.

Many people have wondered why no rescue, partial sale, or bailout was possible for a company that had so much so recently. After all, Osborne Computer Corporation was at its zenith just nine months before it filed bankruptcy. My explanation, based on the foregoing scenario, is that Jaunich had never positioned the company for anything other than a turnaround to occur when he was ready for it. Therefore, following the surprises of late July, he lacked time to implement any other plan. Despite the company's many problems Jaunich introduced no significant cost-cutting programs until early August, after Salomon Brothers had abandoned the private placement. Previous layoffs were merely cosmetic, and month-to-month departmental budgets showed no signs of a company trying to slim down or change course. In my opinion, it all made sense, because until the end of July there was no real reason for the company to change course. I believe that the crisis was of Jaunich's making, and he could just as easily have unmade it.

But it is also possible to explain or rationalize the machinations occurring during the Jaunich regime, reaching a conclusion that Jaunich was simply doing his best.

The purchase of Osborne I inventory, one might argue, was nothing more than an attempt to minimize inventory exposure by buying missing components to complete units for which there already was partial inventory in-house. There was certainly an abundant oversupply of CPU boards. Thus, following the company's bankruptcy, when Jaunich publicly denied buying extra Osborne I inventory in February and March, he might claim that his purchases were simply to avoid scrapping CPU boards. Therefore, they did not constitute purchase of new inventory.

In response to the argument that Jaunich should have been canceling orders wherever possible when Osborne I sales softened in March, one could argue that any wholesale cancellation of orders would have been a knee-jerk reaction. After all, weren't his sales and marketing executives working on a program to revive sales? And what if Executive shipments did slide into June or July? Assuming that the sales and marketing department could revive Osborne I sales, there had to be sufficient inventory to accommodate a resurgence to the sales levels that the company had historically been able to achieve.

On entering the month of April, it could be argued that warning investors and stockholders that Osborne I sales were at a low level would be dangerous and unnecessarily alarming. After all, the Executive was due to be announced in two weeks. If Obsorne I sales simply declined while dealers and customers waited to see the new offering, then it would be reasonable to expect Osborne I sales to revive, assuming that the company had priced the two products correctly. Osborne Computer Corporation needed to borrow additional money. Without the letters of credit the company would have quickly gotten into a cash bind. Was it reasonable to risk such a dangerous situation by turning a sales decline in advance of a new product offering into a cause for alarm?

As for the meeting with the underwriters on Friday, April 22, Jaunich was simply relaying the information he had last received from Jim Ottinger. He was very busy recruiting new executives, preparing for a public offering, and attending the Executive introduction road show. He had no idea that Don Waite, having just joined the company, would deem it necessary to increase reserves so dramatically, and Ottinger had not warned him that April was going to be a financial disaster.

Entering May, Jaunich may have looked with great suspicion on Fred Brown's proposed deals with TWA and Leviton. Fred had not been able to deliver on his forecast for Osborne I sales in March or April, and he was doing no better in May. The company's greatest single asset was its dealer network. Had anyone carefully thought through the impact it would have on the network if Osborne I's by the thousands suddenly appeared on sale at discounted prices outside of the dealer network, further undermining the dealers' ability to unload shelves already choking with slow-moving product? Fred Brown claimed that by the terms of his deals price protection would not be an issue, which is to say that the company would not be required to reduce prices retroactively for dealers who had bought Osborne I's at higher prices within the previous ninety days. But this conclusion was not shared by everyone. Fred Brown, some claimed, was better at making deals than he was at understanding their ramifications. If price protection was an issue, the new dollars brought in might have been significantly offset by a write-down in accounts receivable.

As for reducing the Osborne I price, there would be a large and immediate accounts receivable hit resulting from dealer-price protection, which would have alarmed the banks.

Regarding a private placement of stock, it could be argued that Jaunich was being cautious, and with good cause, by waiting for an audited May year-end statement before allowing Salomon Brothers to proceed. The company's condition was precarious and one letter-of-credit holder was already talking litigation. Would it not be bordering on foolhardy for the company to go hunting for new money with an unaudited year-end statement and the possibility of additional surprises at any moment?

Let's turn to the subject of Jaunich's renegotiated compensation package. Perhaps it did give him a far higher percentage of the company's outstanding stock. But that, one might argue, simply represented the difference between what everyone thought the company was worth in January and what people were assuming it was worth in June. Moreover, it was simply prudent of Jaunich to delay signing a new contract. Reopening negotiations in the face of further deterioration in the company's condition would be extremely difficult. One might argue that Jaunich, had he not been so dedicated, should have quit at the end of April when he discovered the true extent of the company's problems.

But he did not quit. He stayed on and tried to help bring the company out of its problems. Should he be expected to take on this far more horrendous task for a compensation package inferior to the one he had accepted in January? In absolute dollar amounts he was in fact accepting less real cash in July. Twenty-thousand shares sold in March for $80–100 per share was worth more than Jaunich's half-million-dollar bonus plus the retroactive salary increase to $375,000 per annum. And 80,000 shares in January were worth a good deal more than 950,000 shares in July.

Once the underwriters called off the private placement, it could be argued that Jaunich did everything required of a chief executive officer to find a way out from the company's desperate circumstances. He worked with the underwriters looking for a buyer, and he explored the possibility of a last-minute public offering. The company did not file bankruptcy until there was literally no money left. And following the filing of bankruptcy Jaunich remained with the company through its most trying period until a "go-forward" plan was formulated by Ron Brown, which obtained preliminary court approval.

Part III THE AFTERMATH

Chapter Ten AND THEN

The actual filing of bankruptcy on the following Tuesday, September 13, was both an anticlimax and an enormous relief for me. Finally after so many months I was free to act.

The ensuing weeks starkly contrasted my style with that of Jaunich. We both were now free to do our jobs; for months there had been little I could do other than keep the press at bay and prevent internal dissension.

Offers to bail out the company started to pour in. The lunatic fringe was well represented along with serious investors. In every case Jaunich required callers to submit their proposals in writing. If the caller's credentials were not self-evident, these also had to be provided.

ITT vanished from contention, loudly disclaiming that they had ever been interested in Osborne Computer Corporation. An unguarded comment by Jeff Boynton, the company's director of personnel, had caused the ITT story to reach the press. MATRA also disappeared from contention in the following week. The authors of this book do not know what specifically caused these two companies to lose interest.

Sepp Hatzl subsequently claimed that a group of German investors contacted Jaunich with a multimillion-dollar offer of assistance, but gave up with the impression that Jaunich was uninterested in their investment.

Ron Brown (who subsequently developed the go-forward plan accepted by the bankruptcy court) and I both had the impression that Jaunich made no serious effort to help the company out of bankruptcy; in our opinion Jaunich showed no initiative whatsoever. He simply negotiated with creditors and bankers while awaiting any bona fide proposal that arrived unsolicited. He talked to three underwriting firms that specialize in bail-out situations, but they—all three of them—felt there was nothing left to bail out.

Osborne I and Executive sales died out following the filing of bankruptcy. According to John Carson, who for a time remained as part of the post-bankruptcy sales department, it was not the filing of bankruptcy that dried up product demand; in fact, demand temporarily picked up based on lower announced prices. Rather Jaunich for a while stopped all shipments, and then required that legal documents of some complexity be signed by anyone wishing to buy product.

Meanwhile I quickly put together a go-forward plan and called a meeting of interested venture capital representatives. Many came, but more in search of information than out of interest in further investment.

If Jaunich lacked enthusiasm at this point, I operated at the other extreme. I responded to every proposal. The majority were insincere. The most farcical was one Raymond J. Goodsen, who continuously called the company looking for me. Eventually I returned Goodsen's call on Thursday, September 22. He was a wealthy Osborne fan—so Raymond J. claimed—and he had up to $60 million available immediately. He claimed he would provide letters of credit by the middle of the following week.

''Get down to Dallas and we'll meet at the airport right away,'' he urged.

It was too late in the day to verify the man's credentials. I made a few telephone calls that all drew blanks on Goodsen but nevertheless took the midnight flight to Dallas, arriving at dawn. A two-hour meeting was scheduled at the airport, after which I would take the next flight back.

Upon arriving in Dallas, I was met by a very young and very odd-looking fellow, dressed in a dirty, ill-fitting tuxedo. In this garb Goodsen claimed he would fly to New York as soon as the meeting was over to secure go-forward funds for Osborne Computer Corporation. Goodsen's controller was due at any moment with the necessary paperwork to guarantee Osborne Computer Corporation immediate credit. The controller who ultimately showed up wearing blue jeans and a sweatshirt inspired less confidence than his boss in festive garb. Two hours later I returned to San Francisco.

''This character is either the scion of Texas' most hillbilly million-dollar family, or he's a fraud,'' I told Len Weiss, my attorney, when I reached home.

''Sounds like a fraud to me,'' said Len.

''Perhaps so,'' I agreed, ''but what was he up to? He asked for nothing and promised to have a $60-million guarantee by the middle of the following week—all the money that Osborne Computer Corporation needs.''

The fact that Goodsen was weird became apparent later in the day. He called every ten or fifteen minutes stating that the press, having followed him, had overheard the entire airport conversation. Now they were besieging him for a story.

There were eavesdroppers at the adjacent table, all right, but they were from the Plano Texas Narcotics Bureau. A telephone call to Osborne Computer Corporation late that Friday morning was passed on to me at my home.

My wife, Barbara, took the call. She was not at all pleased with my efforts to resume control of Osborne Computer Corporation. In her opinion I was grasping at straws. On receiving the message that the Plano Texas Narcotics Bureau was interested in talking with me about my Dallas airport meeting, she sought me out calling:

"John Z, John Z!"

A very courteous and professional officer who had obviously recorded the entire conversation between myself and Goodsen informed me that Raymond J. Goodsen wasn't the gentleman's real name. The officer assured me that they had spoken with Goodsen, who would not be bothering me again.

"If he does, let us know and we'll knock him on the head," the officer said. "We believe in Texas justice down here."

The most encouraging contact occurred some two weeks after bankruptcy had been filed, when I had called back the visitors from NCR to see how new post-bankruptcy discussions were progressing. I was amazed to discover that NCR had not been approached at all by Jaunich and were in fact waiting for someone to contact them.

By then I had already formulated a go-forward plan, paying out of my own pocket for my attorney to draw up a proposal that Don Waite thought was reasonable and likely to be accepted by the courts. I suggested that the NCR folks simply take over my proposal. Lou Van Antwerp liked the idea, so I flew out to Dayton and Lou gave himself the task of persuading NCR to take over my go-forward plan.

The following Thursday a delegation from NCR visited Osborne Computer Corporation to have a first-hand look at the new, IBM compatible product. I called Jaunich's secretary to advise him of the visit, and stated that I would be there about a half-hour in advance in case anyone wanted an explanation of what was going on.

On arriving, I found that no one was particularly interested in talking about NCR so I settled down to go through accumulated mail. Ten minutes after the NCR group should have arrived I inquired as to whether they had checked in yet and was told that the meeting had already commenced. Going into the Board room I discovered Jaunich conducting a meeting.

"You are welcome to join us," Jaunich said as I walked in.

"You don't seem to understand. This is my meeting and you are welcome to stay if you wish," I replied. Jaunich did not wish to remain. He stalked out of the Board room calling on his executives to leave with him.

Having reviewed important points in my go-forward plan, I escorted the visitors to the research and development area, where the new IBM PC compatible products were to be demonstrated. During the demonstration I visited briefly with some members of the engineering and programming staff who were due to be terminated within a week unless a go-forward plan was accepted by the Board. But the meeting with NCR was interrupted by Jaunich.

"I think it is important that the visitors from NCR understand Osborne speaks only for himself," Jaunich stated, his usual monotone now stiff with barely suppressed rage. "He is not an officer of the corporation and cannot bind the corporation in any way." He then left the room.

Ultimately NCR adopted one small piece of my go-forward plan. They offered to purchase worldwide exclusive rights to the PC-compatible product and the Vixen for $1,300,000. But since that would have gutted the company the offer was not even brought to the Board of Directors.

Putting together pieces of conversation and implied comments, I believe that the plan died largely because of an article by Dan Dorfman that severely undermined my credibility within the financial community. I was privately informed that the story had been planted with Dorfman by Jaunich, but I could not prove it. Jaunich strenuously denied having anything to do with the article.

Whether or not Dorfman was duped into writing the article, it was very uncomplimentary toward me while throwing posies at Jaunich. It discussed my sale of stock in February but did not mention my letter of credit or subsequent purchasing of Series B Preferred shares. It claimed that Jaunich stood alone against a public offering in late April, when in truth the only person even slightly in favor of a public offering was Robert Bily. And it did not mention Jaunich's efforts to see if the company could go public in August. I brought these points to Dan Dorfman's attention via John Eckhouse, a reporter for the *San Francisco Examiner*. I also asked what Dorman thought of Jaunich's wholesale Osborne I inventory purchases during February and March. Dorfman apparently did not care to follow any new leads and dropped the whole thing.

When it became apparent that NCR was not going to support my go-forward program, I fell back on a second source of funding: a San Francisco businessman who had contacted me shortly after news of the bankruptcy hit the press. This gentleman signed a legal letter of intent to provide up to $15 million needed by the go-forward plan. But this gentleman, the black-sheep son of a very wealthy San Francisco real estate development family, terrified Barbara Burdick and my attorneys. An hysterical and incoherent telephone call from this gentleman in the middle of the night convinced me that he was not a reliable partner in any go-forward program, to say the least.

Once I dropped out of the race, Ron Brown picked up the challenge of putting together a go-forward plan for Osborne Computer Corporation. It was logical for Ron to do so, since internationally Osborne had suffered far less than they had domestically. There was still a strong demand for product throughout Europe and South Africa.

First Ron put together a plan in conjunction with Rene Pardeau and his Canadian company, Lanpar. As a customer Lanpar had a dispute with Osborne Computer Corporation. The other creditors were not anxious to see Lanpar escape their disputed obligations. Ultimately Ron Brown had to go forward on his own. Today he is president and chief executive officer of Osborne Computer Corporation. Under his management the company has started building the Osborne I and the Executive again.

Meanwhile I am back together with Georgette Psaris as CEO and executive vice president, respectively, of Paperback Software International, a new start-up.

The major lawsuit filed following Osborne Computer Corporation's bankruptcy was instigated by Ed Shea. It is hard to blame him for being suspicious. In March he bought a block of Osborne Computer Corporation shares from Seymour Rubinstein, paying what is believed to be the highest price ever paid for Osborne shares. Then in August he guaranteed a letter of credit. Within weeks he saw his investments crumble before his eyes.

Arthur Young, Osborne Computer Corporation's auditors, appear to be the principal targets of the law suit. Did they misrepresent the company's condition in November 1982?

One might argue that if the Bank of America turned down Osborne Computer Corporation's request for an increase in line of credit at the very time that Arthur Young was rendering a clean opinion on an audited statement for the company, then the Bank of America saw something Arthur Young should have seen.

I am of the personal opinion that Arthur Young's work was sloppy. On returning from Golden, Colorado, I was so horrified by Jaunich's telephone call that I personally looked into the largest loss item: a $5-million inventory loss attributed to the quarter ending February 1983.

Although I am not an accountant, it seemed evident that a big loss of inventory dollars had to be matched by a loss of physical goods. It took me less than half an hour to do a physical goods inventory balance that highlighted a glaring error in one item, but no significant loss of physical inventory. The question I then posed to the auditors was: "How can there be such a large dollar loss, unmatched by any physical loss?"

The auditors' first answer, a change in inventory valuation, accounted for a few hundred thousand dollars of loss. But for the rest, it was a web of innocent ledger-entry errors and miscoding. A quick nonfinancial calculation could have indicated this web of inaccuracies.

One must conclude that there is more truth than poetry to the old saw: To an accountant the sum of two numbers is any answer you want it to be.

Chapter Eleven THE FUTURE

The trend in high technology is simple. Things are getting smaller, cheaper, more powerful, and more reliable. If we remember those four earmarks, then it is easy to spot the trends once a pattern is established. Computers are getting smaller, as witnessed by the Osborne portable and the TRS-80 Model 100. The newest machines employ more powerful processors that handle more data faster than before. Integrated circuits contain more and more transistors in the same amount of space; they use less energy and are manufactured with techniques designed to lower the costs. It is almost monotonous in its repetitiveness.

While this primary trend affects the technology in general, the marketplace has its own trends that intersect the technological trends. Marketplace trends include the demand for more power at a lessening price, a demand for interchangeability between systems, a demand for upward and downward compatibility, a trend toward ease of use.

These generalities apply to almost every aspect of technology from automobiles to supercomputers. The issues become rather exaggerated in areas where hypergrowth is occurring—specifically the microcomputer industry.

The microcomputer hardware industry does have its own peculiar characteristics. In particular, there is the issue of industry standards. Washing machines and refrigerators do not need industry standards, at least none that a user has to worry about. It is assumed that all appliances use 120-volt alternating current electricity. But the cycle times, door size and other features vary widely. Television sets require more attention when it comes to standards. Europe has different standards for the display than we do in the United States.

Videocassette recorders use incompatible VHS and Beta formats. But when first introduced, there were five or six competing formats—eventually there will be only one. If we remember that the trend is always toward the small and powerful, we have to assume that the videocassette recorder of the future will have cassettes smaller than Beta cassettes with more storage than VHS cassettes. A new 8-mm cassette is on the horizon and it is viewed as the next and final step in the evolution of the technology. It will provide more power in a smaller package at a lower price.

Industry standards within the microcomputer industry are just as important as they were in the record player or video cassette recorder markets. From its earliest days the microcomputer industry has been hobbling toward an industry standard. Between 1975 and 1981 the standard was quite loose. It centered around the 8080 or Z80 microprocessor and the CP/M operating system. Unfortunately each company that used these two elements refused to agree on anything else. Terminals had different ways of controlling cursor movement; diskettes had different formats; parallel ports that communicated to printers were all different.

Even the elementary programming language BASIC varied from manufacturer to manufacturer. It was quite exceptional if a program written for one microcomputer would run on another brand without modification.

Until the advent of the IBM PC no manufacturer large enough to enforce an industry standard ever tried to do so. Apple Computer Corporation could have and perhaps even Radio Shack had the opportunity. But both of these companies had a policy of going their own way and barring all followers.

These issues will at first be muddied by the entrance of AT&T into the computer marketplace. On this point the authors of this book disagree.

Dvorak believes that AT&T, having lived its life as a monopoly, will be unable to compete with IBM and Apple and will either go into a joint venture with Apple or re-emphasize telecommunications, giving up in the microcomputer arena.

Dvorak further believes that Unix, AT&T's operating system, will never become generally popular because it is large, cumbersome, difficult to use, specialized, and unforgiving. Its failure in the marketplace will mark the end of operating systems as an end-user concern. Instead specialized interfaces will be developed to make microcomputers easier to use.

One of the overlooked aspects of both CP/M and PC-DOS, Dvorak believes, was their simplicity. A businessman with no knowledge of computers could easily get a directory listing using the mnemonic command "DIR." It was very easy to use, though not powerful. Unix will finally show the fallacy of thought that feels a complex but powerful operating system is needed or wanted. Screen icons and a pointing device such as a "mouse" will show their appeal in the years to come because they lower the barriers to entry. Unix raises the barrier, which is against the trend.

I agree that the trend will be inexorably toward microcomputers that are easier to use, but my feeling is that the operating system is going to disappear from the end-user's view anyway. Certainly Unix would fail if end-users had to cope with it as they have to deal with MS-DOS today, but in my opinion only programmers will see or use operating systems in the future, and serious programmers generally love Unix. Furthermore, if Unix becomes the next industry standard, and I believe it will, AT&T will be presented with an excellent opportunity to push IBM into second place. Meanwhile, AT&T will enter the marketplace with a copy of the IBM PC, moving on to a Unix-based product at some time in the future.

Microcomputers are no longer high-tech products. They are no more high-tech than are dishwashers or television sets. The winners in the future will be the manufacturers able to build reliable product inexpensively. Westinghouse or General Motors could succeed as easily as any existing computer manufacturer or the Japanese. The microcomputer industry scenario described is made to order for Japan Inc. All that is required of them is that they build an industry standard hardware product, where inexpensive reliability is the key. They will no longer have to worry about software, the one factor that has kept them out of the American market. If their hardware is truly industry standard, it will execute American programs as well as any American microcomputer.

For microcomputer hardware the future therefore belongs to IBM and one or more Japanese manufacturers, along with AT&T if I am to be believed, but not AT&T if Dvorak is correct. Apple will have an ever-harder fight on its hands to stay among the leaders.

From a purely nationalistic viewpoint the American government has no choice but to encourage the dominance of IBM and/or AT&T. Otherwise the market will be dominated by Japan Inc. and there will be no significant American participant.

Despite the fact that a few large companies are likely to dominate the microcomputer hardware industry, there will still be room for a number of small companies. Some of these small companies will succeed by catering to specialized markets that are simply too small to interest the giants. Others will be able to survive simply because the microcomputer hardware business is so large. A company that properly scales its business will be able to operate profitably even if it has one percent or less of the total market.

In sharp contrast to the microcomputer hardware business, it is unlikely that there will be any giants dominating the software market. Nevertheless, the software market will certainly undergo massive changes as it moves from mass confusion to stability.

People who write computer programs have been likened to the authors of books. Accordingly software publishing companies have appeared whose metaphor is the book publisher. Much like book publishers, they receive programs from authors. In exchange for a royalty the software publisher manufactures and distributes manuals and diskettes. But software publishers are far from sweeping the microcomputer software market. This is because the software industry is full of companies backed by venture capital, who sell their products in much the same way a microcomputer hardware manufacturer sells microcomputers.

If the parallel between software publishing and book publishing is valid, then we would have to extend the parallel to the venture capital-backed software product companies that currently dominate the market for microcomputer software. These companies could be likened to a book author who, instead of submitting his manuscript to a publisher, decides instead to self-publish his book and then build a publishing company around his other offerings. Such companies do exist in the world of publishing. My first company, sold to McGraw-Hill, is one. Sybex and Dilithium Press are two others. But there aren't that many compared to the number of software manufacturers, many of whom will soon be out of business.

Why are there so many software companies who have self-published? The answer is that a computer program is a form of intermediate product, more complex than a book manuscript and yet less costly to develop than a piece of computer hardware. Because of this the successful software company of the future will be neither a carbon copy of a book publisher nor a replica of the typical microcomputer hardware company. A probable analogy is an agricultural cooperative such as a fruit packing cooperative. A central company, such as Sunkist, packs oranges and makes orange juice for a large number of orange growers, none of whom would independently have the resources to compete providing their own manufacturing, marketing, sales, and distribution.

Anyone with a manufacturing background can look at the software industry as it exists today and immediately recognize how ripe it is for change. Computer programs today are priced according to a euphemism called "perceived value pricing" which in reality is "extortion pricing." The argument goes that you should pay $500 because as a user it is worth $500 to you. Fair enough, but how many more people are there to whom the program is only worth $100?

In what industry other than the software industry do companies strive to increase the cost of goods as a means of justifying a very high price? The average $500 software packages consist of a manual equivalent to a thin paperback book plus one or two diskettes. This essential part of the product costs a few dollars to manufacture and distribute. But by putting the manual in an expensive-looking three-ring binder and packing the whole thing in a casket-like linen box (which we call "funereal packaging"), it is possible to run up the cost of goods to as high as $50.

Certainly there are industries where some products are packaged expensively so that they will appeal to a snob market. But in the software industry today the overpriced package is the norm.

Software product companies that have self-published their own product will argue that the cost of goods is in fact much higher than stated above, since the cost of product development must be amortized over the units sold. A company that hires innumerable programmers and puts them on the payroll to develop new software products can easily spend $2 or $3 million before the product is ready to go to market. The most optimistic pricing might assume that this development cost is amortized over 100,000 sales, which translates into $30 per software package. But few software packages sell 100,000 copies—not if they retail for hundreds of dollars. So cost of goods has now climbed to anywhere between $80 and $120, enough to justify today's high retail prices.

The flaw in this cost-of-goods pricing is the assumption that software must be developed in a way analogous to hardware by a team of professionals working for a salary. It is in the development of software that the analogy to book publishing becomes obvious. No book publisher would be able to make money selling books at their current rates if they kept authors on the payroll. One might argue that book publishers make their living preying on authors, few of whom make a living from writing books. The average book author, if he or she divides the total royalties received by the number of hours spent on it, will find (from a pure economic viewpoint) more money babysitting. These low-cost hours authors pour into their manuscript as labors of love allow books to be priced as cheaply as they are. And, within limits, the software industry is comparable.

So many talented programmers are willing to pour innumerable hours as labors of love into writing programs that generating new programs with teams of salaried programmers will be uneconomical for many years to come.

Many of the most popular microcomputer programs on the market today were written by one, two, or three programmers. WordStar, VisiCalc, SuperCalc, and Lotus 1,2,3 are examples. Even the trend to integrated software packages leaves the door open to individual programmers. A software publisher can specify and rigidly enforce a few standards such as the use of keyboard and data file structures. If these are followed, then innumerable individual programmers will be able to generate software that works in harmony. Data files created by one program can be accessed by another, and having learned to run one program, the buying public will automatically know how to run any other.

So given the agricultural model, the cost of goods for software is likely to be based on the manufactured cost of the product, with little if any money for product development amortization. Companies that need to include product development amortization in their cost of goods will not be competitive.

Software retail prices will eventually decline. But $500 programs will not be on sale for $50 overnight. One or two attempts at such drastic price reduction have backfired. The buying public was simply unprepared to believe that the $50 product was as good as the $500 product. Instead, as competition builds prices will decline 20–25 percent with each wave of new entries attempting to obtain market share. This can quickly translate into price erosion. Ultimately the price-cutting will stop when it hits the bedrock of product manufacturing costs.

Another argument presented for maintaining high software prices is that the cost of supporting software is very high and must be included in the product retail price. This argument is fallacious. Five hundred dollars is too cheap for any company foolhardy enough to offer free product support with the sale of a computer program. They will quickly go bankrupt, attempting to staff a support department large enough to meet the expectations of a buying public that has been told that it will be supported without limit. Nothing is more economically ruinous than selling a customer a product that appears to be expensive on the promise of receiving some intangible future value. The customer's expectation and the seller's ability to deliver are likely to differ widely. The only economically viable strategy is to eliminate from the price of software any allowance for support and subsequently charge customers a reasonable but profit-making fee for any support they do indeed require. By making support profitable, companies will be encouraged to staff their support departments adequately. And that is far more likely to generate happy customers than a policy of making promises that are economically unachievable.

These low software price levels are significant because they completely change the nature of the software industry and its future participants. An industry dominated by $500 software packages could easily generate a new IBM controlling the lion's share of the market. This is because as long as the product price is high enough for customers to shop carefully they will tend to choose programs with the best-known name. But when the product price is low enough the capriciousness of individual choice comes into play. When people no longer look upon the purchase of software as an investment they will buy based on the design of the cover, the presentation of the manual, or other human factors that have little or nothing to do with the quality of the product or the name of the manufacturer.

This is the most likely future scenario for the software industry. No software manufacturer is ever likely to hold even five percent of the overall market. Just as book publishing has no dominant giant, so there will likely be ten or more front-ranking software publishers in the future with perhaps one hundred second-ranking companies, while the small participants may number in the thousands.

As copy protection techniques become more sophisticated, the piracy problem is also likely to recede. It will never be possible to sell programs on diskette that are uncopyable, but it is already possible to sell programs that can be copied by only proficient and knowledgeable programmers. A tiny percentage of the overall market who copy for their own use are simply not an economic threat. Combined with lower software prices, piracy will eventually be a thing of the past.

So the microcomputer industry of the next decade will consist of inexpensive, powerful, and small machines with easy-to-use software. The software will be inexpensive commodity software. Game software will be like hit records with a weekly "top ten."

IBM will dominate the business hardware business; Apple will maintain its position as a home and personal computer. The Japanese will enter the market and dominate it with the next wave of "lap" computers, products with flatscreen displays that run on batteries and will be introduced in large numbers during the next twelve months.

Software will be the focus of attention from 1990 into the 21st century.

EPILOGUE

Is hypergrowth necessary?

Without question, for Osborne Computer Corporation the answer was yes.

Finite time-windows open for participants in every arena of high technology. The window remains open for a while, then closes. Once the window closes, opportunities for start-ups end.

The microcomputer time-window opened in 1975 when MITS sold its first kit. The window closed sometime in 1983 when IBM had so soaked up unsatisfied demand that hypergrowth pricing models ended (see "A Question of Pricing"). Today no start-up company could succeed in the general microcomputer market. It will be up to the giants to slug it out for market share.

When the time-window opens on a new arena of high technology, the first participants will enter a very forgiving market where demand is so high that an amazing level of corporate sins are forgiven, buried under a welter of orders. Marginal products, slipshod management, cavalier customer and dealer relations, are all forgiven in the face of customers who keep buying because the economic imperative is there, because the product represents good value for money. And they have nowhere else to turn anyway. As the time-window matures the market becomes steadily less forgiving.

Among the early participants the ones who do well are invariably companies who set the pace by sinning less. The companies at the forefront of technology do not come out on top. Newer and better products are unimportant, providing the existing product line is perceived by customers as adequate. That is why Apple Computer Corporation rose to prominence beginning in 1977. Under the expert guidence of Mike Markkula, Apple quickly became the company that sinned the least. They had customer service representatives who could give meaningful answers when competitors had no customer service department at all. They acknowledged defective product and made good on it when such obvious policies were unknown elsewhere. By no stretch of the imagination was the Apple II microcomputer "the best" product technically at any time in its life cycle. For the price the Processor Technology SOL microcomputer was certainly more capable, as were Ohio Scientific's products, or those of Digital Microsystems, Cromemco, or North Star.

If any one man is responsible for Apple Computer Corporation's success it must be Mike Markkula, a fact frequently forgotten by writers and industry watchers with short memories.

The survivors, once the time-window closes on any arena of high technology, are the largest companies and the niche companies. The former do well because they can offer the best prices and support. The latter succeed by addressing markets too small to interest the big guys, and are therefore less price sensitive. To be a survivor in the general market, therefore, you must grow—fast. And the later in the time-window that you enter the market, the faster you must grow, bearing in mind that you are doing so in a steadily less-forgiving environment.

Entering the market late—it was already the summer of 1981—Osborne Computer Corporation had succeeded magnificently by January of 1983. From a standing start, within eighteen months it had grown to become the fourth or fifth largest nonhome microcomputer manufacturer in the world based on month-to-month shipments, the company's rank depending on how one defined a nonhome microcomputer and whose sales figures were believed. And as for customer perceptions, the July 1983 issue of *Office Products* magazine reported Osborne, IBM, and Apple tied in first place among business users of microcomputers as companies that could be counted on. *Consumer Reports* selected the Osborne I as a "best buy." Osborne's dealer network included every respected name in the business: Computerland, Macy's, and Sears, for example. The company had a fiercely loyal network of user groups and a stellar image within every segment of society.

Our speculation that the company's subsequent collapse might have resulted from Jaunich's machinations colliding with bad luck must cloud any postmortem regarding things I did right or wrong as the company grew. But some analysis may be useful nonetheless.

The company's marketing, sales, and public relations programs were an outstanding success. Of that there can be no question.

The company's engineering department was weakly managed; however, by early 1983 it included many strong people. Thus John Hanne was able to turn it into a first-rate operation within months of his arrival. Certainly with a stronger engineering department, earlier, the company could have generated newer products sooner. In particular, if introduced in the summer of 1982, the Executive would have been much more successful; and the Vixen, if introduced in the spring of 1983, would have done very well. In particular an IBM PC compatible portable introduced in early 1983 would have helped a great deal. But the company should only have done less well for lack of these new products; their absence was by no means fatal. Being at the forefront of technology has never created winners in the microcomputer industry, and not being at the forefront of technology had little or nothing to do with the company's difficulties. The most obvious demonstration of this fact is the high sales levels the company achieved during the first quarter of 1983, when the Osborne I was already quite obsolete technically and even competitively.

The company's manufacturing operation was either excellent, a disaster, or somewhere in between, depending on whom you talk to. Certainly the company's manufacturing was not economical in that it was not automated, but automation costs money and we did not have the capital to build a highly automated manufacturing facility. Some of the money raised in a public offering would have been used for this purpose.

To survive in the future, microcomputer manufacturers will have to do their own manufacturing, economically. Handing off manufacturing to a subcontractor will not be possible since the subcontractor has to make a profit. A company that does its own manufacturing does not have to include the subcontractor's profit in his cost of goods, will be able to offer less expensive product, and will take the largest market share. This is why Commodore was the winner in the home computer market during 1983. They did more of their own manufacturing, used fewer subcontractors, and purchased fewer components than anyone else.

Osborne Computer Corporation's financial operations under Ottinger were no shining example for the rest of American industry to emulate; but neither were the company's finances out of control, as has been suggested. The data presented in this book speaks for itself, and those contending otherwise should present evidence, not opinion. The bulk of the reserves created in 1983 reflected Osborne I inventory that should never have been purchased, or other reserves being subjectively increased in the face of a severe net revenue decline.

Turning to staff, systems, and organization, two conflicting influences need to be considered:

1. In the absence of a cohesive organization, people work at cross purposes generating confusion instead of results—which is bad.
2. Within the intoxicating environment of unrestricted and rapid growth, many capable people acquire a will to succeed that borders on missionary zeal. They achieve spectacular results beyond reasonable expectation—that is good.

At Osborne Computer Corporation the entire engineering department prior to John Hanne's arrival represented the most obvious example of confusion. Ottinger's financial group was also weak on organization. But both groups included amazingly strong people. Finance had such stellar performers as Marilyn Johnson, Mike Anthofer, and Bob Lerner. Among the programming and engineering staff Roger Chapman, Wendy James, and Curt Ingraham stand out.

The *Portable Companion* staff and that portion of the customer service organization reporting to Pete Brown achieved the most spectacular results.

In each case the difference between the good and the bad was the quality of management. Simply hiring enough people never solves any problem. Once hired, employees must understand their job and be able to perform it. If the job is ill-defined and the support structure lacking, then one must count on finding a Georgette Psaris or a Pete Brown to create order out of chaos—and that is always a long shot.

In the absence of a Psaris or a Pete Brown, it takes a minimum of three months for new employees to learn their job, so these individuals cannot be used as building blocks in any personnel structure until the three-month learning period has ended. But to be safe, an additional three months is really required to make sure each individual has indeed learned his or her job. And who will make that determination? It has to be someone who has also been through the learning process. Jaunich, unfortunately, was no Psaris or Brown. In my opinion he needed a very full three months to learn his job. But he had been hired as CEO, in which capacity it was he, not we, who determined when he would take over.

The only hope a company has to cope with the organization and personnel problems associated with hypergrowth is to hire overqualified people to begin with and have them institute controls while the company is still far too small to need them. But here is the rub: such overqualified people are the most likely to overregulate, thereby destroying the missionary zeal without which hypergrowth is impossible.

The initial management group early in 1981 was very strong in sales, marketing, and public relations but very weak in engineering, manufacturing and finance. Choosing Tom Davidson as the first executive vice president and general manager was in my opinion a major blunder. But it could not be helped. Davidson was not hired because he was the ideal candidate. More qualified candidates simply did not believe the idea was viable, therefore, they were not interested in the position.

As success brought the company credibility it became quite easy to hire very qualified senior managers, which is where I made my most fundamental blunder. I attempted to hire a replacement for Tom Davidson in 1982, putting off recruitment of badly needed vice presidents until Tom Davidson's replacement had been hired. In early 1982 I could easily have attracted a man as superb as John Hanne to come in and sort out the company's engineering department. I could have strengthened the finance department to eliminate those areas of weakness that were abundantly evident, like the absence of timely financial visibility.

Setting aside the speculation that Jaunich might have indulged in self-serving activities, if any other one thing contributed to Osborne Computer Corporation's downfall it was the very problem Michael Schulhof had identified: the destruction of the will to succeed which, until Jaunich's arrival, had driven the company to its achievements. And the parallel collapse of the company's marketing and public relations programs was devastating because we had relied so heavily on these programs. In retrospect I believe that Jaunich simply did not understand marketing or public relations.

The myth that preannouncing the Executive contributed to the company's collapse has already been dealt with in Chapter 8. There was no preannouncement. And as for new product rumors, I can only reiterate that every company is always working on new products, or they are planning to get out of the microcomputer business. Nothing occurred in March of 1983, as compared to January or February, to kindle significant new product rumors in a manner that so negatively impacts the company's sales. Rather, it was the end of a major sales promotion with nothing to follow that caused the sales collapse.

But a question one might well ask is, ''What the heck was I doing during the amazing sequence of events beginning in April 1983? Why didn't I stand up and fight?''

The answer is simple. In February, March, and April I knew I would never get along personally with Jaunich, but I remained impressed with his credentials and his intellect. I doubted my judgement, not his, on all subjects save the purchase of excess Osborne I inventory, and I genuinely believed that issue was taken care of at the February Board meeting.

I had no basis for being suspicious of Jaunich's motives, so I had decided that it would be in the stockholders' interests if I left the company in Jaunich's hands to run it as it grew. I spent a lot of time traveling on goodwill tours to help the company's public relations efforts and worked at securing the company's future products. Between the beginning of February and the end of April, I traveled from February 19 to February 26, from March 8 to March 14, and from March 28 to April 13.

Certainly I must be criticized for spending so much time away from the office in this sensitive transitory period, but my major concern was to avoid unnecessary friction with Jaunich, who even by late February had adopted an aloof and hostile attitude toward me and the original managers.

I was faced with the choice of fighting, with the self-evident accusations that I never intended to give up control at all, or I had to make way. I chose the latter course. Following the April crisis I still believe that I had no choice other than to sit tight and not make waves. After all, until late July the overwhelming probability appeared to be a rescue. Perhaps I could have fired Jaunich and taken control back, but to keep the underwriters interested—and that was an utter necessity—I would have had to convince them of Jaunich's malevolence. That was unlikely then, considering that it is something I cannot do conclusively today, even after many months of research.

But the undeniable fact remains: I turned my company over to Jaunich and did not fight back when I saw it going down.

Appendix A SUMMARY OF PURCHASE ORDERS

rw = rework
vr = vendor reject
rev. = revision

	January			February			March			April Status Balance to Be Shipped at End of March		April to June	
	PO#	Quantity	Price	PO#	Quantity	Price	PO#	Quantity	Price	Quantity	PO#	Quantity	Price
Ingress													
Part Number 3P11042-00							CSR8169240	2129	11390		CSR5179	209	418
Part Name bezel, front							3–4 vr				4–6 rw		
Part Number 3P11042-00							CSR8169170	555	2959		CSR5170	54	108
Part Name bezel, front							3–4				4–12 rw		
Part Number 3P11042-00				CS8166618	2200	4400				2200	CSR6489	309	618
Part Name bezel, front				2–18	rw						4–12 rw		
Part Number 3P11042-00							CSR6527	553	1106		CSR5101	237	474
Part Name bezel, front							3–4 rev. J				4–15		
Part Number 3P11042-00							CSR4091	2129	4258		CSR2220	86	172
Part Name bezel, front							rw 720				5–6 rw		
Part Number 3P11042-00							CS8169510	5000	37700	4000	CSR85466	22	44
Part Name bezel, front							3–23				5–6 rw		
Part Number 3P11042-00	CS8158468	12776	96331								NSR20041	16	32
Part Name bezel, front	1–24										6–9 rw		
Part Number 3P11042-00							NS815827B	19412	146366	4480			
Part Name bezel, front							3–16 rev. J						
Both O1&E													
Part Number 3P11037-00							CS816958	33900	312898	25900			
Part Name case, bottom							3–11						
Part Number 3P11037-00							NS816959D	4500	23075	1000			
Part Name case, bottom							3–15						

rw = rework
vr = vendor reject
rev. = revision

	January PO#	January Quantity	January Price	February PO#	February Quantity	February Price	March PO#	March Quantity	March Price	April Status Balance to Be Shipped at End of March Quantity	April Status Balance to Be Shipped at End of March PO#	April to June Quantity	April to June Price
Part Number 3P11037-00	CS815839B	11053	102019										
Part Name case, bottom	1–24 rev. D												
Part Number 3P11037-00	NS815834B	16095	148557							5280			
Part Name case, bottom	1–24 rev. D												
Part Number 3P11037-00							CSR8169240	879	3533				
Part Name case, bottom							3–4 vr						
Part Number 3P11037-00							CSR8169170	1002	8587				
Part Name case, bottom							3–4						
Part Number 3P12035-00				CS8166618	2000	4000				2000			
Part Name bezel, keyboard				2–18 rw									
Part Number 3P12035-00							CSR6527	291	582				
Part Name bezel, keyboard							3–4 rev. J						
Part Number 3P12035-00							CSR4091	249	498				
Part Name bezel, keyboard							3–4 rw						
Part Number 3A11030-00							CSR8169170	2	4				
Part Name pocket, handle							3–4						
Part Number 3A11038-00							CSR8169170	1059	10654				
Part Name case, top							3–4						
Part Number 3A13034-00							CSR8169170	552	4455				
Part Name chasis, assy							3–4						
Part Number 3P11039-00							CSR8169170	35	21				
Part Name cover, cord							3–4						
Part Number 3P12035-00							CSR8169170	291	701				
Part Name bezel, keyboard							3–4						
Part Number 3P12036-00							CSR8169170	261	1224				
Part Name case, keyboard							3–4						
Part Number 3A11038-00							CSR8169240	758	7626				
Part Name case, top							3–4 vr						

Part Number 3A13034-00				CSR8169240	14	113	
Part Name chasis, assy				3-4 vr			
Part Number 3P12035-00				CSR8169240	245	600	
Part Name bezel, keyboard				3-4 vr			
Part Number 3P12036-00				CSR8169240	348	1632	
Part Name case, keyboard				3-4 vr			
Part Number 3A11032-00				NS816960C	2000	19960	
Part Name case, top				3-16			
Part Number 3P12036-00				NS816949D	1400	6510	1400
Part Name case, keyboard				3-16			
Part Number 3P12035-00				CS816950D	34750	83400	28750
Part Name bezel, keyboard				3-11			
Part Number 3A13034-00				CS816952	7600	62397	4100
Part Name chassis, assy				3-11			
Part Number 3P11040-00				CS816953D	31400	19468	24900
Part Name cover, vent				3-11			
Part Number 3P11041-00				CS816954D	32400	46008	21400
Part Name pocket, cord				3-11			
Part Number 3A11030-00				CS816955D	7500	15600	4500
Part Name pocket, handle				3-11			
Part Number 3P11039-00				CS816957D	33700	20557	24300
Part Name cover, cord				3-11			
Part Number 3A11038-00				CS816961D	33400	333412	26400
Part Name case, top	NS815826B	20170	1613	3-11			
Part Number 3P11043-00	1-24						18970
Part Name knob fab							
Part Number 3A13034-00				NS815828B	17082	140243	2750
Part Name chassis, sub				3-16 rev. B			
Part Number 3P12036-00	NS315829B	17412	80967				11330
Part Name case, keyboard	1-24 rev. F						
Part Number 3P12035-00				NS815830B	18146	43550	2900
Part Name bezel, keyboard				3-16 rev. G			
Part Number 3P11041-00				NS815831B	17076	24248	10550
Part Name pocket, cord				3-15 rev. F			
Part Number 3A11030-00				NS815832B	19360	36108	12050
Part Name pocket, handle				3-15 rev. A			

rw = rework
vr = vendor reject
rev. = revision

	January			February			March			April Status Balance to Be Shipped at End of March		April to June	
	PO#	Quantity	Price	PO#	Quantity	Price	PO#	Quantity	Price	Quantity	PO#	Quantity	Price
Part Number 3A11038-00 Part Name case, top	NS815833B 1–24 rev. A	16880	168462							11330			
Part Number 3P11039-00 Part Name cover, cord							NS8158358 3–15 rev. E	17331	10572	10050			
Part Number 3P11040-00 Part Name cover, vent							NS815836B 3–15 rev. C	18984	11769	10550			
Part Number 3P11040-00 Part Name cover, vent	CS815837B 1–24 rev. C	11080	6869										
Part Number 3P11039-00 Part Name cover, cord	CS815838B 1–24 rev. E	8665	5286										
Part Number 3A11038-00 Part Name case, top	CS8158405 1–24 rev. A	12032	120080										
Part Number 3A11030-00 Part Name pocket, handle	CS8158418 1–24 rev. A	11120	23130										
Part Number 3P11041-00 Part Name pocket, cord	CS8158428 1–24 rev. F	10208	14495										
Part Number 3P12035-00 Part Name bezel, keyboard	CS8158438 1–24 rev. G	9704	23290										
Part Number 3P12036-00 Part Name case, keyboard	CS8158448 1–24 rev. F	10520	48918										
Part Number 3A13034-00 Part Name chassis, sub	CS8158458 1–24 rev. A	12260	100655										
Part Number 3P11043-00 Part Name knob fab	CS8158478 1–24	9860	789										
Part Number 3A11043-00 Part Name knob, assy							CS816968D 3–23	35550	2844	16550			

January Orders Canceled in March							
Part Name							
Part Number 3P11039-00	CS8158508	25850	15768	CS8158608	25850	15768	
Part Name cover, cord	1–24			3–7			
Part Number 3P10037-00	CS8158618	17930	238596	CS8158818	17930	238596	
Part Name case, bottom	1–24			3–7			
Part Number 3P11040-00	CS8158638	17930	16028	CS8158638	17930	16028	
Part Name cover, vent	1–24			3–7			
Part Number 3A11038-00	CS8158558	25850	257984	CS8158558	25850	257984	
Part Name case, top	1–24			3–7			
Part Number 3P11041-00	CS8153568	25850	36708	CS8158568	25850	36708	
Part Name pocket, cord	1–24			3–7			
Part Number 3P11043-00	CS8158578	25850	1468	CS8158578	25850	1468	
Part Name knob fab	1–24			3–7			
Part Number 3P12035-00	CS8158588	25850	62040	CS8158588	25850	62040	
Part Name bezel, keyboard	1–24			3–7			
Part Number 3P12037-00	CS8158598	25850	120202	CS8158598	25850	120202	
Part Name case, keyboard	1–24			3–7			

---

both O1&E

Oak							
Part Number 7A02005-00	CSR812276	410	11316				
Part Name keyboard	2–14 rw						
Part Number 7A02005-00	CSR811902	270	7452				
Part Name keyboard	2–14						
Part Number 7A02005-00	CSR816389	50	1380				
Part Name keyboard	2–14 rw						870
Part Number 7A02005-00	CSR816354	870	22925				
Part Name keyboard	2–2						68
Part Number 3A10060-01				CSR6525P	68	1360	
Part Name array, keyswitch				3–10			106
Part Number 7A02005-00				CSR6587	106	2120	
Part Name keyboard				3–18			

rw = rework
vr = vendor reject
rev. = revision

		January			February			March		April Status Balance to Be Shipped at End of March		April to June	
	PO#	Quantity	Price	PO#	Quantity	Price	PO#	Quantity	Price	Quantity	PO#	Quantity	Price
Part Number 3A10060-01							CSR5102	150	3000				
Part Name array, keyswitch							3–18 rw						
Part Number 3A10060-01							CSR6584	43	860				
Part Name array, keyswitch							3–21 rw						
Part Number 3A10060-00							CS8176008	12500	236876				
Part Name array, keyswitch							3–29						
Part Number 3A10060-00													
Part Name array, keyswitch													
Testology													
Part Number 3A10063-00				CS813975	11	1827							
Part Name main, cpu				2–18									
Part Number 6B10011-01	CS815906	57000	1203840							150			
Part Name pcb, rev. A	1–21 rev. A												
Part Number 3A03004-00	CS815907	39000	1074840							43			
Part Name disk, elect	1–23									10500	CS8176158	14000	227400
Part Number 3A10063-00	CS815908	22100	3955900								4–5		
Part Name main, cpu	1–21 rev. K										CS819022	14838	281029
Part Number 3A03004-00	CS815909	22000	176000								6–27		
Part Name disk elect	1–21 rev. M									11			
Part Number 6N00001-01	CS815233A	29600	1250008										
Part Name pcb, rev. A	1–19 rev. A									45000			
Part Number 3A03004-00				CSR815254	340	2464							
Part Name disk elect (rework)				2–1 rw						31000			
Part Number 3A02011-00	CS815256	3000	495540										
Part Name main logic	1–19 rev. P									15000			
Part Number 3A02011-00	CMR815257	5000	50000										
Part Name logic, rev. P	1–28 rev. P									17384			
Part Number 3A10063-00	CMR815258	1000	6000										
Part Name cpu, rev. K	1–28 rev. K									24600			

Part Number 3A02011-00	CSR815260	3100	31000										
Part Name main logic	1-31 rev. P									32			
Part Number 3A10063-00				CS815278	11	1827							
Part Name main cpu				2–22						10000			
Part Number 6N00001-01				CM815279	782	1193							
Part Name pcb				2–22									
Part Number 3A03004-00							CS815280	10000	284600				
Part Name disk elect							3–15						
Part Number 3A10063-01													
Part Name array, keyswitch													
Zenith													
Part Number 7P80320-00				CS813874	5780	289731							
Part Name 5, vidio				2–4									
Astec													
Part Number 7A02014-00							CS816697B	8000	220880				
Part Name power supply							3–17						
Part Number 7A02014-00							CS816697B	2000	55220	3500			
Part Name power supply							3–17						
Siemans Forestlane													
Part Number 2A00064-XX							NS813979	4500	333000		CS818927	39	6598
Part Name drive							3–9				5–25		
Part Number 2A00064-XX				CS816007	400	2350				5700			
Part Name drive				2–10									
Part Number 7A03002-00	CSR816303	80	5760										
Part Name drive	1–17												
Part Number 2A00064-XX				CSR816319	480	4725							
Part Name drive				2–10									
Part Number 2A00064-00				CSR816390	600	43200							
Part Name drive				2–14 rev A & rw						2000			

rw = rework
vr = vendor reject
rev. = revision

	January			February			March			April Status Balance to Be Shipped at End of March		April to June	
	PO#	Quantity	Price	PO#	Quantity	Price	PO#	Quantity	Price	Quantity	PO#	Quantity	Price
MPI													
Part Number 2A00064-XX		rework		CSR810054	569	45520							
Part Name drive				2–14 rw						80			
Part Number 2A00064-XX				CSR816361	20600	1606800							
Part Name drive				2–12 rev. A									
Part Number 2A00064-XX				CSP816352	548	43200							
Part Name drive				2–17									
Kagadenshi													
Part Number 7P80320-00				CS811987	5200	249600							
Part Name 5, monitor				2–22									
TEC													
Part Number 7A02005-00				CS815216	21000	196890			19320		CV20129	27	108
Part Name keyboard				3–2							6–27		

	January	February	March	April to June
Total $ for O1 only:	8345219	2296837	1294369	8572
Total $ for O1 or Exec:	845130	47073	1497065	227400
Total $ ordered in January and canceled in March:	748794		748794	
Total $ for O1 in Feb and March:	3591206			
Total $ for O1 or Exec in Feb and March:	1544138			
Total $ for O1 and O1 or Exec in Feb and March:	5135344			

Appendix B COMPLETE FINANCIAL STATEMENTS

Osborne Computer Corporation
Consolidated Statement of Operations
Year Ended November 28, 1981
(thousands of dollars)

Net sales			$5,761
Costs and expenses:			
Cost of sales		$3,878	
Marketing		960	
Research, development and initial production costs		1,282	
General and Administrative		832	
Interest, net		91	7,043
Net loss	(1,282)		
Accumulated deficit, at November 29, 1980	(38)		
Accumulated deficit, at November 28, 1981	(1,320)		

Osborne Computer Corporation
Consolidated Statement of Changes in Financial Position
Year Ended November 28, 1981
(thousands of dollars)

Sources of working capital:	
Common stock issued or issuable	$3,142
Borrowings under bank line-of-credit	1,375

Total sources		4,517
Applications of working capital:		
Operations:		
Net loss	$1,282	
Depreciation, a charge not requiring working capital	(52)	1,230
Additions to property and equipment		769
Increase in other assets		77
Advance royalty payments, non-current portion		194
Working capital deficiency at November 29, 1980:		
Cash	(16)	
Note payable to company president	51	35
Total applications		2,305
Working capital at November 28, 1981		$2,212

Osborne Computer Corporation
Consolidated Balance Sheet
November 28, 1981
(thousands of dollars)

Assets		
Current Assets:		
Cash and short-term cash investments		$75
Accounts receivable, less allowance for doubtful accounts of $124,000.(note 3)		2,016
Inventories (note 3):		
Purchased parts and work-in process	$2,686	
Finished goods	148	2,834
Prepaid royalties		297
Other prepaid expenses		45
Total current assets		5,267

Property and equipment, at cost:		
Assembly and test equipment	380	
Office furniture and equipment	332	
Automobiles and trucks	55	
Leasehold improvements	6	
Total property and equipment	773	
Less accumulated depreciation	47	726
Prepaid royalties, less current portion (notes 2 and 5)		194
Other		70
Total assets		$6,257

Liabilities and shareholders' equity	
Current liabilities:	
Accounts payable	$2,644
Accrued compensation and related expenses	217
Other	194
Total current liabilities	3,055
Borrowing under bank line-of-credit (note 3)	1,375
Shareholders' equity:	
Common stock, no par value; 2,000,000 shares authorized; 238,239 shares issued and outstanding; 9,150 shares issuable (note 4)	3,147
Accumulated deficit	(1,320)
Total shareholders' equity	1,827
Total liabilities and shareholders' equity	$6,257

Osborne Computer Corporation

Consolidated Statement of Operations

Year Ended November 27, 1982

(thousands of dollars)

Net sales (note 7)	$68,783
Costs and expenses:	
Cost of sales	50,795
Research and development, including initial production costs in 1981	1,643

Marketing	12,745
General and administrative	3,531
Total costs and expenses	68,714
Operating income (loss)	69
Interest expense	1,090
Net loss	$(1,021)
Net loss per common share (note 1)	(.39)
Common shares used in computing per share amounts	2,602

Osborne Computer Corporation

Consolidated Statement of Changes in Financial Position

Year Ended November 27, 1982

(thousands of dollars)

Applications of working capital: Operations, net loss	$1,021
Depreciation, a charge not requiring working capital	(443)
Total working capital used by operations	578
Additions to property and equipment	4,865
Advance royalty payments, noncurrent portion	1,033
Reduction of obligations under capital leases	108
Increase in other assets	179
Total application of working capital	6,763
Sources of working capital:	
Sale of preferred stock	9,938
Common stock issued or issuable, net of additions to shareholder notes receivable	418
Net borrowings under bank credit line	7,504
Additions to capital lease obligations	730
Total sources of working capital	18,590
Increase (decrease) in working capital	11,827
Increase (decrease) in components of working capital:	
Current assets:	
Cash	422
Accounts receivable	9,129
Inventories	15,823

Prepaid royalties	410
Other prepaid expenses	148
Total current assets	25,932
Current liabilities:	
Accounts payable	11,566
Accrued compensation and related expenses	507
Capital lease obligations due within 1 year	108
Other accrued liabilities	1,924
Total current liabilities	14,105
Increase (decrease) in working capital	11,827

Osborne Computer Corporation
Consolidated Balance Sheet
Year Ended November 27, 1982
(thousands of dollars)

Assets	
Current assets:	
Cash	$497
Accounts receivable, net of allowance for doubtful accounts of $352,000 ($124 in 1981) (note 2)	11,145
Inventories (note 2)	
Purchased parts	7,454
Work-in-process, including parts at subcontractors	8,637
Finished goods	2,566
Total inventories	18,657
Prepaid royalties	707
Other prepaid expenses	193
Total current assets	31,199
Property and equipment (note 3):	
Assembly and test equipment	2,767
Office furniture and equipment	815
Leasehold improvements	2,056
Total property and equipment	5,638
Less accumulated depreciation	490

Net property and equipment	5,148
Prepaid royalties, less current portion (notes 1 and 6)	1,227
Other assets	249
Total assets	$37,823

Liabilities and Stockholders' Equity	
Current liabilities:	
Accounts payable	$14,210
Accrued compensation and related expenses	724
Capital lease obligations due within one year	108
Other accrued liabilities	2,118
Total current liabilities	17,160
Bank credit line (note 2)	8,879
Capital lease obligations (note 3)	622
Commitments and contingencies (note 6)	
Shareholders' equity (note 5):	
Preferred stock, no par value, liquidation preference of $150 per share; 100 shares authorized; 66,667 shares issued and outstanding	9,938
Common stock, no par value; 500,000,000 shares authorized; 2,825,892 shares issued and outstanding (2,473,890 in 1981)	4,460
Accumulated deficit	(2,341)
Total	12,057
Less shareholder notes receivable	(895)
Total shareholders' equity	11,162
Total liabilities and shareholders' equity	$37,823

Appendix B

Osborne Computer Corporation

Income Statement

Quarter End February 1983

(thousands of dollars; before adjustments)

	Actual	Budget	Act. B/(W) Budget
Gross revenue			
Computers	$32,970	$27,237	$5,733
Software	1,465	1,673	(208)
Other	2,950	3,056	(106)
Total	37,385	31,966	5,519
Deductions	(3,008)	(4,031)	1,023
Net revenue	34,377	27,935	6,442
Cost of sales	23,797	18,454	(5,343)
Gross margin	10,580	9,481	1,099
% of net revenue	31%	34%	
Expenses			
Marketing	7,475	5,568	(1,907)
Engineering	1,700	1,331	(369)
Gen. & Admin.	1,530	1,024	(506)
Interest & Other	520	699	179
Total	11,225	8,622	(2,603)
Profit before tax	(645)	859	(2,603)
% of net revenue	(2%)	3%	

Variance Analysis

Budgeted PBT	$0.9M
Actual variances (PBT impact)	
Unit volume (24K vs. 19.0K budget)	2.2
Revenue deductns. (Budget is maximum)	1.0
Spending—Manacturing	(0.6)
Operating and other	(1.2)
Promotions	(1.4)
Inventory adjustments	(0.8)
Other COGs (rework)	(0.7)

Total variances	(1.5)M
Actual PBT	(0.6)M

Osborne Computer Corporation
Balance Sheet
Quarter Ending February, 1983
(thousands of dollars)

	Actual	Budget	Actual B/(W) Variance
Current assets			
Cash & S.T. investments	$ (859)	$ —	$ 859
Accounts receivable			
Trade	15,250	15,298	48
Other	418	398	(20)
Reserve	391	459	68
Net accounts receivable	15,277	15,237	(40)
Inventories			
Gross	16,686	18,054	1,368
Reserves	312	812	500
Net inventories	16,374	17,242	868
Prepaid royalties	1,870	2,088	218
Other prepaids	102	173	71
Total current assets	32,764	34,740	1,976
Long-term assets			
Property & equipment			
Gross PP&E	8,867	8,815	(52)
Accum. depreciation	836	779	57
Net property & equipment	8,031	8,036	5
Other assets	403	347	(56)
Total long term assets	8,434	8,383	(51)
Total assets	$41,198	$43,123	$1,925

Liabilities			
Accounts payable	12,400	14,200	1,800
Accrued liabilities	6,886	4,947	(1,939)
Notes payable	450	—	(450)
Total current liabilities	19,736	19,147	(589)
Bank borrowings	11,493	10,741	(752)
Shareholders' equity			
Preferred stock	9,937	10,183	246
Common stock	5,641	3,473	(2,168)
Retained earnings	(2,742)	(421)	2,321
Shareholders' Receivables	(2,867)	—	2,867
Total shareholders' equity	9,969	13,235	3,266
Total liabilities and shareholders' equity	$41,198	$43,123	$1,925

Osborne Computer Corporation
Consolidated Statement of Operations
Twelve month periods ended February 26, 1983 and February 27, 1982
(thousands of dollars)

	1983	1982
Net sales	$92,789	$15,413
Cost and expenses:		
Cost of sales	70,668	12,153
Product discontinuance costs (note 1)	4,295	—
Research and development	3,618	1,276
Marketing	19,848	1,971
General and administrative	5,088	1,146
Interest expense	1,355	206
Total costs and expenses	104,872	16,752
Net loss	(12,083)	(1,339)
Net loss per common share (note 1)	(4.47)	(.68)
Common shares used in		

computing loss per share	2,705	1,972

Osborne Computer Corporation
Consolidated Statement of Changes in Financial Position
Twelve month periods ended February 26, 1983 and February 27, 1982
(thousands of dollars)

	1983	1982
Applications of working capital:		
Operations net loss	$12,083	$1,339
Depreciation, a charge not requiring working capital	(647)	(90)
Total working capital used by operations	11,436	1,249
Common stock repurchased	544	—
Additions to property & equipment	7,555	1,341
Advance royalty payments, noncurrent portion	$1,285	$260
Reduction of obligations under capital leases	240	—
Increase (decrease) in other assets	(6)	374
Total applications of working capital	21,054	3,224
Sources of working capital:		
Sale of preferred stock	9,938	—
Common stock issued or issuable, less net additions to shareholder notes receivable	253	3,146
Additions to capital lease obligations	1,414	—
Total sources of working capital	11,605	3,146
Decreases in working capital	(9,449)	(76)
Increase (decrease) in components of working capital:		
Current assets:		
Cash	651	(28)
Accounts receivable	7,342	6,288
Inventories	6,135	5,282
Prepaid royalties	727	131
Other prepaid expenses	6	15

Total current assets	$14,861	$11,688
Current liabilities:		
Bank overdraft	498	1,012
Bank credit line	8,116	3,337
Accounts payable	10,205	6,824
Accrued compensation and related expenses	(70)	363
Capital lease obligations due within one year	205	—
Note payable to company president	—	(7)
Other current liabilities	5,356	197
Total current liabilities	24,310	11,766
Decrease in working capital	$(9,449)	$(78)

Osborne Computer Corporation
Consolidated Balance Sheet
Years Ended February 26, 1983 and February 27, 1982
(thousands of dollars)

Assets	1983	1982
Current assets:		
Cash	$ 651	—
Accounts receivable, net (notes 4&5)	13,638	$ 6,296
Inventories (note 5):		
Purchased parts	3,450	4,025
Work-in-process, including parts at subcontractors	5,359	1,065
Finished goods	2,608	192
Total inventories	11,417	5,282
Prepaid royalties	858	131
Other prepaid expenses	22	16
Total current assets	26,586	11,725
Property and equipment (note 7):		
Assembly and test equipment	1,549	626
Office furniture and equipment	4,055	681
Leasehold improvements	3,308	50

Total property and equipment	8,173	1,265
Less accumulated depreciatation	739	92
Net property and equipment	8,173	1,265
Prepaid royalties, less current portion (notes 3 and 10)	1,545	260
Other assets	427	433
Total assets	$36,731,000	$13,683
Liabilities and Shareholders' Equity (Deficit)		
Current liabilities:		
Bank overdraft	$1,510	$1,012
Bank credit line (note 5)	11,493	3,377
Accounts payable (note 1)	17,128	6,923
Accrued compensation and related expenses	293	363
Capital lease obligations due within one year	$205	—
Other current liabilities	5,553	$ 197
Total current liabilities	36,182	11,872
Capital lease obligations (note 7)	1,174	—
Commitments and contingencies (notes 10 and 11)	—	—
Shareholders' equity (deficit) (note 9):		
Series A Preferred stock, no par value, liquidation preference of $150 per share; 1,000,000 shares issued and outstanding	9,938	—
Common stock, no par value; 110,000,000 shares authorized; 2,942,645, shares issued and outstanding (2,551,640 in 1982)	5,888	3,402
Accumulated deficit	(13,674)	(1,591)
Total	2,152	1,811
Less shareholder notes receivable	(2,777)	—

Total shareholders' equity (deficit)	(625)	1,811
Total liabilities & shareholders' equity	$36,731	$13,683

Osborne Computer Corporation
Income Statement
Quarter Ending May 28, 1983
(thousands of dollars)

	Actual	%	Forecast	%
Net revenue	$21,985		$20,000	
Cost of sales	17,395	79.1	15,600	78.0
Gross margin	4,590	20.9	4,400	22.0
Operating expenses				
Marketing	9,565	43.5	8,400	42.0
Engineering	2,225	10.1	2,000	10.0
G&A	2,835	12.9	2,300	11.5
Total	$ 14,625	66.5	$12,700	63.5
Operating loss	(10,035)	(45.6)	(8,300)	(41.5)
Interest	578	2.6	477	2.4
Other income & expense	597	2.7	223	1.1
Net loss	(11,210)	(50.9)	(9,000)	(45.0)
Contingency	—	—	1,000	5.0
Net loss before OCC-1 reserve	(11,210)	(50.9)	(10,000)	(50.0)
OCC-1 reserve	3,500			
Net loss	(14,710)			

Osborne Computer Corporation
Balance Sheet
Quarter Ending May 28, 1983
(thousands of dollars)

Assets	
Cash	$(143)
Accounts receivable	10,511

Inventories	15,944
Prepaid royalties	999
Other prepaid expenses	172
Total current assets	27,483
Property & equipment	
Assembly and test equipment	4,267
Office furniture and equipment	1,976
Leasehold improvements	3,781
Total property & equipment	10,024
Accumulated depreciation	1,306
Net property & equipment	8,718
Prepaid royalties, less current portion	2,123
Other assets	313
Total assets	$38,637
Liabilities & Shareholders' Equity	
Bank overdraft	—
Subordinated notes payable	$350
Bank credit line	18,593
Accounts payable	25,800
Accrued compensation	747
Capital leases, current portion	396
Other accrued liabilities	7,433
Total current liabilities	53,319
Capital leases	940
Shareholders' equity (deficit)	
Preferred stock	9,938
Common stock	5,773
Accumulated deficit	(28,490)
Total shareholders' equity	(12,779)
Less shareholders' notes	(2,843)
Total shareholders' deficit	(15,622)
Total liabilities & shareholders' equity	$(38,637)

Appendix B

Osborne Computer Corporation

Consolidated Balance Sheet

May 28, 1983

(thousands of dollars)

Assets	
Current assets:	
Accounts receivable, net (notes 4 and 5)	$10,452
Inventories (notes 1 and 5)	7,761
Purchased parts	3,174
Work-in-process, including parts at subcontractors	3,174
Finished goods	4,981
Total inventories	15,916
Prepaid royalties	999
Other prepaid expenses	172
Total current assets	27,539
Property and equipment (note 7):	
Assembly and test equipment	3,088
Office furniture and equipment	3,155
Leasehold improvements	3,781
Total property and equipment	10,024
Less accumulated depreciation	1,306
Net property and equipment	8,718
Prepaid royalties, less current portion (notes 3 and 10)	2,028
Other assets	622
Total assets	$38,907

Liabilities and Shareholders' Equity (Deficit)	
Current liabilities:	
Bank overdraft	$226
Bank credit line (note 5)	17,843
Notes payable to vendors (note 1)	3,750
Accounts payable (note 1)	21,954
Accrued compensation and related expenses	1,497
Capital lease obligations due	

within one year	396
Other current liabilities (note 6)	8,602
Total current liabilities	54,268
Capital lease obligations (note 7)	940
Commitments and contingencies (notes 10 & 11)	—
Shareholders' equity (deficit)(notes 9 & 13):	
Series A Preferred stock, no par value, liquidation preference of $150 per share; 1,000,000 shares authorized; 66,667 shares issued and outstanding	9,938
Common stock, no par value; 110,000,000 shares authorized; 2,943,225 shares issued and outstanding	5,897
Accumulated deficit	(29,383)
Total	(13,548)
Less shareholders' notes receivable	(2,753)
Total shareholders' equity (deficit)	(16,301)
Total liabilities and shareholders' equity	$38,907

Osborne Computer Corporation
Consolidated Statement of Operations
Twelve month period ended May 28, 1983
(thousands of dollars)

Net sales	$104,759
Costs and expenses:	
Cost of sales (note 1)	88,181
Research and development	5,917
Marketing	27,940
General and administrative	7,585
Interest expense	1,590
Total costs and expenses	131,213
Net loss	(26,454)
Net loss per common share (note 3)	(9.55)
Common shares used in computing loss per share	$ 2,771

Appendix B

Osborne Computer Corporation

Consolidated Statement of Changes in Financial Position

Twelve month period ended May 28, 1983

(thousands of dollars)

Applications of working capital:	
Operations, net loss	$26,454
Depreciation, a charge not requiring working capital	(1,137)
Total working capital used by operations	25,317
Common stock repurchased	544
Additions to property and equipment	8,092
Advance royalty payments, noncurrent portion	1,894
Reduction of obligations under capital lease	474
Increase in other assets	460
Total applications of working capital	36,781
Sources of working capital:	
Sales of preferred stock	9,938
Common stock issued, less net additions to shareholder notes receivable	286
Additions to capital lease obligations	1,414
Total sources of working capital	11,638
Decrease in working capital	25,143
Increase (decrease) in components of working capital:	
Current assets:	
Accounts receivable	6,857
Inventories	(560)
Prepaid royalties	647
Other prepaid expenses	(53)
Total current assets	$6,891
Current liabilities:	
Bank overdraft	(915)
Bank credit line	6,851
Notes payable to vendors	3,750

Accounts payable	12,002
Accrued compensation and related expense	1,497
Capital lease obligations due within one year	396
Other current liabilities	8,453
Total current liabilities	32,034
Decrease in working capital	$25,143

Glossary KEY PEOPLE

Jerry Anderson President of Two Pi Corporation.
Lou Van Antwerp NCR engineering manager.
Mike Anthofer OCC Finance Department.
Greg Belange Bank of American representative.
Tony Bergis Member of OCC Board.
Robert Bily Member of OCC Board.
Dennis Bovin Salomon Brothers employee.
Jeff Boynton Director of Human Resources, OCC.
Dan Bricklyn Co-author of VisiCalc.
Dan Brown OCC programmer, fixed bug in CP/M BIOS.
Fred Brown Director of National Accounts, OCC.
Pete Brown Customer support, OCC.
Ron Brown VP International, OCC.
David Bunnell Founder of early *Personal Computer* magazine.
Barbara Burdick Public Relations Specialist, OCC (Osborne's wife).
David Carlick Head of David Carlick Advertising, OCC's advertising agency.
George Carr VP Operations, OCC.
Rolf Carrick Osborne distributor in Sweden.
H. "Bert" Carson VP Human Resources, OCC.
John Carson OCC employee, in sales/marketing.
Roger Chapman OCC programmer, helped fix bug in CP/M BIOS.
Dan Costa Director of QA, OCC.
Ben Counter Fictitious name for first OCC financial professional.
Fred Coury Engineering consultant.
Adrianna Crow Bank of America representative.
Tom Davidson OCC original general manager.
Dan Dorfman Syndicated columnist.

Jack Dulaney Member of the firm of Smith Barney.
John Dvorak Co-author of this book.
John Eckhouse *San Francisco Examiner* writer.
Gordon Eubanks Author of programming language CBASIC.
Lee Felsenstein Designer of the Osborne I.
Richard Frank Author of SuperCalc, president of Sorcim.
Bob Frankston Co-author of VisiCalc.
Paul Freiberger Writer for *InfoWorld* magazine.
Mark Garretz Microcomputer engineer.
Bill Gates Owner of Microsoft, a software company.
Don Geyer Summer 1983 controller and VP, OCC.
Bill Godbout Owner of CompuPro.
Raymond J. Goodsen Man saying he would bail Osborne out.
Richard Graham President of OCC Australia.
Lynn Hagen Original OCC staffer, designed the original dealer program.
John Hanne VP Engineering, OCC (1983).
Sepp Hatzl President of Osborne, Germany.
Mike Healy President of Osborne, Great Britain.
Thom Hogen Software Acquisitions Director, OCC.
Les Hogan Silicon Valley founding father, ex-chairman of Fairchild, member of OCC Board of Directors.
Porter Hurt Owner of PH Components and Testology.
Mike Iannamico Documentation writer, OCC.
Curt Ingraham Engineer, OCC.
Portia Isaacson Owner of Future Computing.
Wendy James OCC Programming and Engineering staff member.
Robert Jaunich President and CEO of OCC.
Steven Jobs Chairman, Apple Computer Corporation.
Knut Johansson Osborne distributor in Norway.
Marilyn Johnson Finance department, OCC.
Bob Jones Publisher of *INTERFACE AGE* magazine.
Tad Kruzeweics Owner of Computique computer chain.
Martti Laine Osborne distributor in Finland.
Eric Larson Writer for *The Wall Street Journal.*
Bob Lemon Production manager, OCC.
Bob Lerner Receivables manager, OCC.
Bob Leviton Surplus goods dealer.
Pat McGuire Engineer, OCC.

Mike McCullough Director of Domestic Marketing for OCC, who then transferred to International Operations.

Bill Mallard Founder of IMSAI and Computerland.

Bernard Maniglier Osborne distributor in France.

Mike Markkula Director of Apple Computer Corporation in its early days.

Bob Marsh Designed first double density upgrade for Osborne I.

Jack Melchor Venture capitalist, OCC Board member.

Dave Miller Made European versions of Osborne I.

Bob Moody Manager of Osborne software group.

Ron Ogg Manager of Osborne software group.

Adam Osborne Narrator of this book.

Ken Oshman OCC Board member, president of Rolm Corporation.

Fred Osowick Head of service organization, OCC.

Jim Ottinger Head of finance, OCC.

Rene Pardeau Owner of Lanpar, Canadian Osborne distributor.

Bent Petersen Osborne distributor in Denmark.

Jerry Petruzzelli OCC attorney.

Jerry Pournelle Science fiction writer, microcomputer industry columnist.

Georgette Psaris VP Marketing, OCC.

Ed Richter VP Engineering, OCC.

Ed Roberts MITS founder.

Seymour Rubinstein Chairman of MicroPro, OCC Board member.

Joseph Roebuck VP Marketing, OCC.

Michael Schulhof Presidential candidate for OCC, President of SONY America.

Ed Schaeffer Writer for *The Wall Street Journal.*

Ed Shea Filed lawsuit after bankruptcy.

Clive Sinclair English computer designer.

Les Solomon Former editor of *Popular Electronics* magazine.

Juggi Tandon Founder of Tandon Magnetics.

Marlene Tanner Administrative Assistant, OCC.

Annette Truesdell Customer Relations Manager, OCC.

Tom Unterman OCC attorney, outside.

Bruce Van Natta IMSAI employee.

Donald Waite Chief Financial Officer, OCC.

Jim Warren Computer Faire founder.

Len Weiss Osborne's personal attorney.

Stan Wilkendorf Osborne representative in Hong Kong.
Malcolm Williams Hired by OCC to troubleshoot.
Steve Wozniak Designer of the Apple II.
Gerald Wright Owner of Digital Deli, first Osborne dealer.